'Between the road to Mandalay and Route 66, slightly to the east of Suez and west of the yellow brick road, following the second star to the right just to the borders of the land of lost content, on a clear day you'll see Mornington Crescent, that corner of a wireless field which is forever Camden, those snowy woods by which even Humph's horse gives his harness bells a shake, the sunny side of any radio street'
Gillian Reynolds, *Daily Telegraph*

'When I first played Mornington Crescent I thought it was akin to playing water polo. Without the polo. With the benefit of age, wisdom and youthful ignorance, I realise now that it is more like chess for the mind'
Paul Merton

'Mornington Crescent is a puzzle wrapped in an enigma that would've baffled even the formidable brainpower of Bletchley Park'
Terry Ramsay, *Evening Standard*

'If you've understood Mornington Crescent, nothing else in your life makes sense'
Jeremy Hardy

'A simple game, always played to the standard I would expect'   **Sandi Toksvig**

'Mornington Crescent is a true metaphor for life: long silences punctuated by pointless chatter, illogical journeys and maniacal laughter'
Justina Vaughan, New King's Road, London

ACKNOWLEDGEMENTS

The authors would like to acknowledge the assistance of The All-England British Mornington Crescent Federation, the National Mornington Crescent Archives, the Royal Mornington Crescent Legion, Mornington Crescent Anonymous, the London Transport Games Museum (Inverness), Holsten Breweries plc, the Image of the Moving Museum, Londontran Sport, Spellcheck, Jane Route, Endeavour Trellis, Colin Dale, Virgin Drains, and the Mornington Crescent Staff Social Club, without whom this book might have been a great deal better.

For her unflagging patience, invaluable support, understanding and tolerance, the authors would also like to express gratitude to their wife, Elaine.

THE LITTLE BOOK OF

MORNINGTON CRESCENT

by Graeme Garden, Jon Naismith & Iain Pattinson

not to mention
Tim Brooke-Taylor, Barry Cryer & Humphrey Lyttelton

ORION

An Orion paperback

First published in Great Britain in 2000
by Orion Media
This paperback edition published in 2001
by Orion Books Ltd,
Orion House, 5 Upper St Martin's Lane,
London WC2H 9EA

Second impression 2002

A CIP catalogue record for this book
is available from the British Library.

ISBN 0 75284 422 9

Photographs by kind permission of:
Hulton Getty Picture Library, London's Transport Museum,
The V&A Picture Library

Design and layout by Essential Books

Printed and bound in Great Britain by
Clays Ltd, St Ives plc

LIST OF CONTENTS

Isle of Eriska Hotel, Ledaig, Oban, Argyll, PA37 1SD

Total pages (including this one): 1   *From:* DAME JUDI DENCH.

Message:
....

As a lifelong player of Mornington Crescent I wholeheartedly recommend this book which will hopefully reveal once and for all the startling simplicity of this endlessly fascinating game and dare I hope put an end to the endless correspondence and early morning telephone calls from Mrs Trellis of North Wales.

I shall never forget the excitement of my first move between Totteridge and Cockfosters, when Bartlett's Pass was imposed, during a particularly vicious game in the Green Room at the Old Vic in 1957.

It wasn't until I toured West Africa in January 1963 that I realised how influential the game had been in uniting such diverse cultures and it reminded me of the exchange between Stanley and Livingstone when the immortal line "Doctor Livingstone I presume?" was answered by a hesitant "Tooting Broadway...?"

I must say I am surprised and saddened that this epic confrontation has been omitted from the book.

But as long as Mornington Crescent remains in the expert hands of Humphrey Lyttelton, Barry Cryer, Stan More, Paul Merton, Theydon Bois, Sandi Toksvig and Dolli Shill, we can be assured that future generations will continue to be fascinated by this intriguing game.

Judi Dench

Page 6 stunna Dame Judi has five 'O' levels, likes to travel, and is hoping one day to run her own hairdressing salon.

Dear Dame,

Thank you for taking the trouble to write. The publishers have sent me a copy of your notelet by e-male, and I have read it twice. I was sorry to see that you were surprised and saddened by the book, but I know exactly what you mean. However I am thrilled to find that you and I have in 'Mornington Crescent' a shared experience. We all remember the first time we came across the game, in the same way that everyone can remember where they were when Nigel Kennedy's accent was murdered, when Buzz Armstrong conquered Mount Eveready with Sherpa Transit, or what we were doing when England scored the winning the goal in the 1966 World Cup Final (I am no football fan, in fact I was only there because my Russian boyfriend at the time was employed as a linesman). Regular as clockwork, for a few minutes on a Sunday afternoon, or a Monday evening, or three o'clock on a Thursday morning (repeated the seventh Wednesday after Lent on Long Wave only, subject to Focus Group Snooker Schedule confirmation), a nation shares this common love of the Grand Game.

What excites me more than anything else is that I now have your address, and I look forward to being your pen-friend.

Yours in haste

      Mrs Trellis

      North Wales

MORNINGTON CRESCENT
THROUGH THE AGES
THE TALE OF A TUBE STATION IN PICTURES

The end of the line at Mornington Crescent, as it was in 1864. Passengers completed their journeys to and from Edgware by coach.

The old lift at Cryer's Junction, now replaced by a pipeline.

The Chief Steward welcomes passengers aboard the dining car at Mornington Crescent station. One regular traveller is reputed to have taken lunch on the train to Collier's Wood every single day for 37 years. His name is believed to have been J. H. Lewisson, but sadly no picture of him survives.

Testing the top speed of the 'up' escalator, 1919.

Mornington Crescent Station [exterior] in 1930. Interestingly, the men pictured on the pavement outside are plain-clothes police officers, staking out an illicit lager brewery operating behind a 'front' on the rented upper floor. The ground floor tobacconist's shop is also a 'front': Angel, Botibol & Co were, in fact, a firm of bootleg solicitors.

One of the many small fake Mornington Crescent stations erected around London during the Blitz to confuse enemy bomber pilots. This structure also doubled as a public convenience, at the request of the customers of the chemist's shop next door. Incidentally, two of Angel, Botibol & Co's clients can be seen waiting outside, hoping for some last-minute business under their 'To Let' sign.

Fare dodging was rife – even in the 1950s.

Photograph of passengers at Mornington Crescent, recovered from the battered camera of the late C. W. Pimms, 1959.

The booking hall at Mornington Crescent after its makeover by Lawrence, Llewellyn, Bowen, and Associates. Note the MDF barriers installed by Handrew and Andrew Construction. The clean lines are sadly disfigured by a 'Malicious Damage' sign, planted outside the booking office by vandals.

In the 1970s, following a campaign by feminists, tickets for the ladies' could at last be obtained from the liftman.

Following a campaign by feminists, the title 'liftman' was changed to 'liftperson'. Here the liftperson is seen mischievously hiding from approaching ladies!

A young Tim Brooke-Taylor falls foul of the Northern Line's strict dress code, 1974.

MORNINGTON CRESCENT
A HISTORY OF THE GAME
PART 1 **ROMAN TIMES**

NO ONE knows for sure when the game called
'Mornington Crescent' was devised, nor by whom.
All we do know with certainty is that a game was
being played regularly by the Romans before the
invasion of Britain which they called 'Non iguato
Cresseunt' ('I shall not be a crestfallen iguana').
A competition quite so reliant on arithmetical syntax
as Mornington Crescent undoubtedly might be
considered by some to be, would surely have been
beyond the Romans due to their idiosyncratic method
of counting. For example, they had no numerals as we
know them, and relied instead on a series of letters to
represent them, but with no particular logic. One was
'I', five was 'V', ten was 'X', 50 was 'L', 100 was 'C',
500 was 'D', and so on all the way up to 1,000, which
was some other letter. Thus, our fifteen (15) becomes
IV, which in Rome was four, whereas twenty-five (25),
which should be IIV, was in fact XXV and the sum of
the two was XL (or, in our terms, the second cheapest
specification of Ford Cortina). However, the Romans
knew that XV plus XX equals XXLIV (a smaller
number than XL) or, in our terms, 1,010,515. You
don't have to be Herbert Einstein to see what effect
this has on even the simplest, Standard Game (and to
any Roman soldier who went out on a Friday night
with 500 Denarii and came back with 495). Another
effect of having small numbers larger than big ones
was that the Romans were forced to count backwards,

which explains why Julius Caesar first invaded Britain in 55 BC and then returned a year later in 54 BC. The inability, for example, to declare Seven Dials other than after anywhere containing the number eight or higher renders the game almost unplayable. From this, we can conclude without fear of contradiction.

Cleaning work at Mornington Crescent in 1953 reveals a Roman mosaic clearly outlining a primitive diagonal.

As the above picture so clearly illustrates, a very basic form of the game was laid out in mosaic form as early as the 2nd century AD, probably for the amusement of British servants. Sadly, the place names were removed as a wartime emergency measure and were never released under the 30-year rule.

GREAT PLAYERS OF THE GAME
BROTHER CHALFONT [520–560 AD APPROX.]

LITTLE is known of Chalfont's early years, save that he was noviced and installed at Kirkstall Abbey during the Abbotage of Father Rosaenominus in the early sixth century. It is supposed that, following his departure from the abbey, he travelled widely as an Itinerant Brother, spreading the Good Word and the Received Rules throughout southern Britain, living on the charity of the good people who purchased his dusters, dish-mops and oven gloves. He worked diligently as a missionary, and most notably converted the people of Dollis Hill to Christianity by impressing them with the number of pictures of the Angel Islington he could engrave on the head of a pin.

The Tractus Monkorium of Brondesbury records that 'Chirpy Challie' Chalfont settled eventually at the Monastery of St Ockwell in the Northwood Hills, where he was appointed brother attendant to the Poisons Garden, a post which had unexpectedly fallen vacant. His many hours spent in the library gained him an encyclopaedic knowledge of the Encyclopaedia, and his surviving illuminated manuscripts demonstrate that he was the first to record and define the 'True and Onlie Rules of the Grate Gayme'. His miraculous Hermit's Abasement from Snaresbrook to Boston Manor is as perfect a Gridiron Slip today as it was then. Respect for Brother Chalfont's knowledge and authority brought him many admirers, most notably St Giles, who often visited him during the holidays.

His contributions to the game might have faded into obscurity, had they not been rediscovered in the sixteenth century by Bishop Hugh Latimer. The bishop became a stout defender of Brother Chalfont's legacy, to the extent that he publicly opposed Henry VIII's Act of Six Articles, which directly contravened Chalfont's Regulae Ruislipii, and the unfortunate Latimer was declared a heretic and burnt at the stake. A cathedral was secretly erected to the memory of Chalfont and Latimer, and can still be seen today, having been converted for use as a tube station in 1923.

§§ §§ §§ §§

LETTERS TO THE CHAIRMAN: 1

Dear Mr Lyttelton,

I must bring to your attention a scandalous fraud recently perpetrated on myself. Imagine my dismay on removing the enclosed wrapper, believing I had at last purchased a set of rules for the much-loved tube station game, only to find four part-baked Gallic breakfast rolls.

Yours faithfully,

P. B. Stanbrook

Tiverton, Devon

● *How sad that you gave up your search for the rules so easily. Did you not think to break open the rolls and examine their contents?*

Humph

Dear Sir,

<u>Mornington Crescent</u>

Observations recently taken from Westminster Bridge suggest that the London game will shortly undergo a

massive rule change when the new tunnel for the Jubilee
Line allows Eurostar trains to travel to Green Park on
alternate Fridays.

Yours sincerely,

Wallace McMillan
Bebington, Wirral

● *I'm afraid you appear to have an incomplete grasp of
Penegar's Principles of Congruence. However, it's kind
of you to take an interest in the game. Keep trying!*
Humph

Dear Mr Lyttelton,

As a keen player of 'Mornington Crescent', I feel that
Samantha Close (photograph enclosed) would be an ideal
addition to the game. Perhaps points could be awarded on
the basis of how close
the contestants get to
Samantha.

Yours sincerely,

Hugh Meteyard
Theydon Bois, Essex

● *Thank you for the
enclosed photograph,
which sadly appears
to be a fake, as there is no mention of a 'Samantha Close'
in the excellent* London Street Guide *compiled by Wilfred
Atoz in 1947. Could this be something of a 'leg-pull' on
your part? The name 'Meteyard' would seem to give the
game away.*
Humph

THE RULES OF
MORNINGTON CRESCENT
A MASTERCLASS FOR BEGINNERS

It is safe to assume that even the most inexperienced beginner will have a sound working knowledge of the basic rules of the Straight Game, so we shall waste no time on them here.

The Board and Pieces

On opening the brightly but helpfully decorated box, you will find nestling inside it the Board, the Pieces, and a Booklet. Tip them out on to a flat surface, and familiarise yourself with them in the usual way.

● The Board has four edges: Topside, Rightbottom, Leftbottom, and Wing. Arrange the board so that the Topside faces the Dealer, if there happens to be one present. The square playing surface is divided into a grid consisting of 83 identical squares. [As squares 66, 13, 47 and 49 are only used during Advanced Shunts, they are almost invariably ignored.]

● The six enamelled Bakelite Pieces are in the form of: one dachshund, one catapult, one bishop, one Aga oven, and two potatoes. This is their correct order, unless Hopkins' Constrictions are applied. Each piece has a value of 0.27p.

● The booklet contains some hints on pronunciation, 'Appendix A', and a list of recommended snacks for the Long Game. In it you will also find a useful list of addresses from which replacement booklets may be purchased.

Generally speaking, the Board, Pieces, and Booklet will only serve to confuse the players, and are best discarded at this stage. Please, as always, dispose of them thoughtfully. Once they are out of the way . . .

. . . YOU ARE READY TO PLAY MORNINGTON CRESCENT!

The BBC's Board of Governors enjoy a game while waiting for their wives.

The Teams
Each side consists of two to 13 teams, of at least one player each.

The Captains [and Other Ranks]
The Team Captain is selected by throwing a dice – whoever it hits is the chosen Leader. The Captain then appoints the Lieutenants, Petty Officers, Senior Conductors, and so forth. This depends, of course, on

the size of the teams. For example, very short players make poor Sergeants. You will soon get the hang of this.

Territories

No team of more than two players is allowed to declare Territories, and this applies to teams of two or fewer players as well.

Clothing

Clothing should be comfortable and smart, especially the skirt or trousers. It is important that sleeves and socks should not restrict gestures. Hats are permitted, but only one per head.

The Opening

Once all players are in position according to the Constantine Deployment. . .

. . .YOU ARE READY TO PLAY MORNINGTON CRESCENT!

The End Game

The so-called End Game begins with the first move. This sounds a great deal more complicated than it is. The first move, also known as the opening gambit, *le Jeu d'Engagement*, or *das Erstschlachtschlage*, is made by the player to the left of the Trackholder, and play then progresses alternately to the right and left. Other players may of course interrupt this progression, but only in strict sequence. Incidentally, inexperienced players are often confused by the number of first moves available, and find themselves dithering, which loses points. It is usually safe to begin with a blot above the Line, and over the years Putney Bridge has proved to be a pretty solid banker.

Once the Primary has been enstaked, and accepted without prime challenge, [McCawdle's], play continues, *pet-à-pet*, and only ends when one of the players is in a position to bag 'Mornington Crescent' itself. Play is then over. With these simple basics in mind . . .

. . . YOU ARE READY TO PLAY MORNINGTON CRESCENT!

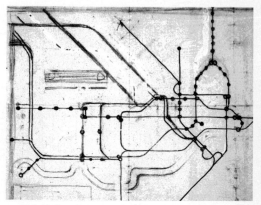

H. C. Beck's early underground draft, known as Draft Becks.

Advanced Play

The first rule of Mornington Crescent is quite simply 'Don't try to be too clever!' That having been said, there is a great deal of fun to be had, and many points to be scored, from taking advantage of some of the finer aspects of High Play, and the novice should not be afraid of 'chancing his or her arm or leg' by giving it a go.

Progression

Play advances by means of progression, by which is meant a logical sequence of moves or 'strikes'. To put it simply, 'Mornington Crescent' is an <u>organic</u> game, and this is best illustrated by analysing a typical contest. In this case we consider a game played *'à plaisaunce'* during an inter-county final in 1997. Do not be misled by the players' evident high spirits!

White – 'Goodge Street'

An unremarkable opening, typical in cautious Front-Game play, but not without its perils, as it leaves White's partners' South East completely exposed.

Brown – 'Queensway'

Brown is planning a set-up here [possibly a Luxemburg Shift], looking to develop a Quadrant which opens all three Diagonals below the line.

Green – 'Fairlop'

This smashing volley brings the score to Deuce.

Aubergine – 'Oh...Euston Road'

Caught on the back foot, Aubergine makes an unforced error, and the game is practically given away. If, instead of boxing out the F, J, O and W placings, he had parleyed Euston Square, this would have drawn the opponents into an elliptical progression. As it is, the Western approaches are opened, and White pounces.

White – 'Oxford Circus'

White is quick to capitalise on the poor positional play, and consolidates an already-strong Outer Ring.

Brown – 'Pimlico'

An elegant response, making the Triple Helsinki available, and opening up Rear Access to Suburban Bidding.

Aubergine – 'Albemarle Street'

This player seems to have given up, and this clumsy move breaks both Tangents. However, the Inner Circle has not yet been declared, and no players are yet on Grue's Probation, so there is life in the game yet!

Yellow – 'St Martin's Lane'

The sacrifice of St Martin's Lane is a clever piece of Quartering here, and had it been made earlier, it might have led Brown into a trap.

White – 'Hammersmith Broadway'

A curving Loop Shift [not one for the amateur!]. In fact, White has carelessly placed the team in Nip without realising it. Luckily, no damage done.

Brooke-Taylor – 'Mornington Crescent!'

Where did that come from?

If you follow these moves on the diagram, you will find everything falls into place.

YOU ARE READY TO PLAY MORNINGTON CRESCENT!

The Offside Rule

There is no more hotly disputed yet widely misunderstood aspect of the Game than the Offside Rule. However, as 'Nosey Parker' [the Mornington Crescent Tipster of the *Independent on Sunday*] puts it so succinctly, 'If it weren't for the Offside Rule, there would be nothing to prevent a player from declaring "Mornington Crescent" on his or her *opening move!* This would end the game at a stroke, and might deprive the players of much of their fun.' For this reason alone, the Offside Rule is of importance, and should be memorised.

Remember: if a player moves to such a location that there are less than two occupied bases between the location played and the next but one Shift Zone, Morton's Convention being in play, whether the Loop has been vectored from either Diagonal or not, and all other players are out of Nip, then that move is declared under-struck, and therefore void, meaning that the player has no option but to offer a Bakerloo Redress, and be declared out of line and off order, and must miss a turn.

This should not be confused with the Offside Rule.

Scoring

Devotees are proud of the fact that Mornington Crescent is the only game still played which has a Binary Scoring System. Those unfamiliar with the principles of Binary Arithmetic are advised to consult the excellent 'HM Customs and Excise Pamphlet 5867 – Arithmetic, Binary, Principles of' by Knoeppfler and Hoogstratten [HMSO 7/6d]. Applying a basic rule of thumb, the system can be summarised thus:
The Winner scores 1, everyone else scores 0.

Summary

Well there you have it. Simple, really, isn't it? One final point: before embarking on a life-long and passionate devotion to the Great Game, and pitting your wits against Crescenteers of experience and guile, ask yourself this question:

ARE YOU SURE YOU ARE READY TO PLAY MORNINGTON CRESCENT?

GREAT PLAYERS OF THE GAME
NICHOLAS LYMMPE [1649–1656]
The Infant Repository

DURING Cromwell's Parliament the Game was deemed an offence against the State, punishable by death. This was partly due to the Puritans' stand against any form of fun, but also because the Game contained so many coded references to the Crown – King's

Nicholas Lymmpe with his head supported by his head supporter.

Cross, Queensway, Royal Oak, and so on. Nicholas Lymmpe showed a remarkable flair for the game [his first word was 'Dagenham'] and by all accounts was born with a fully developed and encyclopaedic knowledge of all the moves and rules. Unfortunately he was given to blurting out a sequence at moments when Cromwell's spies might be about, and his family was therefore obliged to keep him in a tin box for the rest of his young life. However, it is thanks to the Infant Repository of all things Morningtonian that the Great Game survived the Parliamentarian suppression. The tin box can be seen in the Metal Box Company museum at Aldgate.

MORNINGTON CRESCENT
A HISTORY OF THE GAME
PART 2 **THE DARK AGES**

WHEN the the Romans left Britain, it descended into what became known as the Dark Ages, presumably because they took all their Roman candles with them. Consequently, the playing of Mornington Crescent fell out of fashion until what became known as the Middle Ages, although no one called them the Middle Ages at the time, because the ages afterwards hadn't happened and, as no one could read Latin (which was why there were no doctors), they had little idea anything had happened before, so there was nothing to be in the middle of. So it was, that the word 'Now' was invented and the game we call 'Mornington Crescent' can be directly traced to this period. The game played by those who had served the Romans was generally known as Roman Tun Crescent (a 'tun' being a unit of measurement which developed into the Metric Tunne). However, as any Britons who had worked for the Romans were in danger of having their heads shaven and being tarred and feathered, anyone who could play the game lived in fear of being automatically assumed to have been a collaborator and so certain codes were devised. The widely held theory is that, instead of 'Roman' Tun Crescent, it became 'Now' Tun Crescent, and whenever the question was asked 'What shall we play?', in a secret acknowledgement that the game had been played before, the cry would go up, 'More Now Tun Crescent', which in time became corrupted into

Chaucer's characters check out the Canterbury gyratory system.

'Mornington Crescent'. Widely held the theory may be, but does it hold water?

The answer may be found in another theory, i.e. that these players regarded themselves as an elite sect, not accountable to the normal rules of law and happy to push themselves ahead of other members of society, rather like modern-day cyclists. They were a xenophobic, misogynistic, self-serving bunch bound by arcane rituals involving weird, brightly coloured items of clothing. They met in secret lodges called 'golf clubs', many of which have survived to modern times. As none of our (female) researchers has managed to penetrate this dark, mysterious world, we are left totally unable to examine exactly what game they play, but it almost certainly isn't Mornington Crescent.

A TASTE OF
MORNINGTON CRESCENT
Finger-wiping fun in the kitchen!

TUFNELL PORK

A popular and economical dish for those unexpected occasions.

Ingredients

4–5 sheets of skag-end of belly pork

37–39 teaspoonsfuls of pork stock or cream

1 medium plum

half a double-sized onion

Method

Marinade the ingredients in a large earthenware *pot de cochon* overnight. Cook in a medium oven [or cook twice in a small oven]. Drain off the liquid and thicken with anything to hand. Garnish with scratchings and serve.

PARSON'S GREENS

A healthy and economical dish to serve when unwelcome guests drop in.

Ingredients

spinach, cabbage, lettuce, peas, beans, kale, etc.

green beetroot

water

Method

Heat 'n' serve.

EAST HAM

A quick and economical variation on a traditional Beacontree favourite.

Ingredients

1 haunch of ham, trussed and passed as fit for human consumption

3 litres of oak smoke

Method

Release the ham from its truss, and – voilà!

BRENT CROSS BUNS

A seasonal and economical addition to any jumble stall.

Ingredients

225g/8lb self-raising salt

a pinch of flour

3 tbsps [from the Tbspsina region of Hungary if possible]

half a basin of caster sugar

a generous handful of black pepper

1 large sultana, diced

Method

Bake in a Delia Bun-Master.

Shrink-wrap in polythene. Slip into cardboard box, suitably decorated. Seal in Nail-Prufe Cellophane.

Stamp best-before date on bottom [of box!].

Sell.

SHEPHERD'S BUSH PIE

A traditional and economical regional dish for the ungrateful guest.

Ingredients

1 kilogram [imperial] of mutton, freshly cut from a pre-cooked sheep
6 eating potatoes
1 packet of instant carrot
1 frozen onion
3 parsleys
a cupful of wet breadcrumbs
lemon grass and jalapeño peppers to taste

Method

Line a baking dish with pastry. Mince the eels and haddock together with the turnip, and form into 'torpedos'. Spit-roast over a barbecue [mark 7]. Prepare the custard separately, and serve tepid.

ELEPHANT AND CASSEROLE

A tasty and economical way to use up those menagerie leftovers.

Ingredients

elephant scraps
juice of half a lemon
nutmeg
thyme
1 small turnip
37 other small turnips
many onions

Method
Simmer ingredients together over a low heat for 2–3 days, stirring occasionally. Serve with celery sticks.

COQ FOSTERS
Follow any good recipe for 'Coq au vin', but in place of wine use lager.

NOTTING HILL GATEAU
A nourishing and economical addition to the tea-table.

Ingredients
8oz plain flour
8oz attractive flour
1 knob of sugar
1 tub of healthy-alternative butter substitute
chocolate flavouring E194837542
3 eggs [Scotch]
6 anchovy tails

Method
Beat the ingredients together in a bowl. Pour into a cake tin or bucket. Brûle with a Gary-Pro Blo-torch. Steam over a bain-marie, pricking every 35–40 seconds. Turn out when cold. Slice and serve with buttered pickles.

BON APPETIT!

THE SCANDAL OF 'MAD JACK' CAMDEN
A Curious Sidelight on the History of the Game

Sir John, 'Mad Jack' Camden was a noted Regency fop and notorious gambler. His family home was the original Chalk Farm Estate, to the north of London. The farm itself once supported a fine flock of Aberdeen Angus pigs, and was one of the first agricultural establishments to breed a strain of baby spinach acceptable to the delicate palates of the Ladies at Court.

Jack's father, Sir William 'Mad Bill' Camden had inherited the estate from his father, Richard, 'Mad Dick' the Milkman, of Kentish town. Sadly, by the time Sir William 'Mad Bill' died, the flocks and poultry herds had dwindled to a handful of otters and but a single breeding pair of Ptarmigans. The vast old kitchen garden had long since gone to seed, and the vast old kitchen gardener had long since gone to sea. The farm's sole income now came from the drilling of a meagre seam of chalk, which went to supply the schoolmasters at Harrow. When Sir John, 'Mad Jack' and his wife Elizabeth, 'Dim Betty' and their seventeen children (from the 18-year-old Jeremy, 'Mad Jeb', to the infant Eglantine, 'Mad Baby') took over the estate there was precious little left of value, and what there was, Mad Jack squandered at the notorious gaming tables of Primrose Hill.

So it was that upon one fateful night, while Dim

Betty stayed at home, chopping furniture and throwing it on to the fire in a pathetic attempt to keep cool, Mad Jack found himself slipping through the portals of 'The Golden Nougat', High Class Confectioners and Gambling Den, just off Fitzroy
Road. The proprietor, Asmodeus Turnpickle, welcomed him with a sly wink, and ushered him through to the smoke-filled back room, where the blaze was soon under control. As the fumes cleared, Jack Camden was hardly surprised to see that one of the tables was occupied by none other than the Prince of Wales, known to his intimate circle as 'Vinny'. The Prince was a man of generous proportions, which was why none other than he sat at the table – there wasn't room for anyone else.

Draining his bumper of sweet sherry, the Prince beckoned for Mad Jack to come closer, while calling for more wine and crisps for the company, as he played a merry jigot on his banjo, and blew up a handful of party balloons.

'Do ye not join us, Mad Jack?' roared His Royal Highness, 'We are grown weary at Whist, and seek stimulation of a more convivial nature to sharpen our senses dulled with liquor and nibbles.'

'Might I venture a round of Mornington Crescent, sir?' ventured Jack Camden.

'Hurrah,' said the assembled company.

Among their number Jack recognised the familiar figures of the Beaux Brummel, Nash, and Bridges, one of the Wedgwoods, a few Chippendales, the Duke of Wellington, Capability Llewellyn Bowen, and Christopher Biggins, plus a hundred or more others whose name badges had fallen off.

'Gad's Withers!' bellowed Prince George. 'Did I not always tell ye that when 'tis a matter of frolic, Mad Jack's yer man? Hop lively to it! Hazoo!'

Quick as thought, the tables were dragged into a circle, then arranged as an octagon, again as a letter W, and then finally piled up in a corner and forgotten. The jolly company arranged themselves into two and a half teams, and chose the three required captains apiece. Jack found himself directly opposite His Royal Highness, and gave a solemn bow. The Prince acknowledged Jack's gesture by wiggling his ears, and then wiggling his own.

The appointed referee was Dr Johnson, justly famed for inventing with his brother, another Dr Johnson, the well-known Baby Powder. 'Just add water!' it said on the packet. The referee blew his whistle, and dropped a pomegranate to indicate 'Game on'.

'Hanover Rules!' shouted the excited Prince, so Hanover Rules it was. The Duke of Devonshire was first out of the slips.

'Euston Square,' he announced in measured tones.

'Earl's Court!' expostulated the Prince.

'Wigs!' cried Mad Jack, and once the forfeit had

been paid amidst mounting merriment, the game continued.

'Fairlop,' offered Tom Rowlandson, returning to his sketchbook with a weary chuckle.

'Earl's Court!' countered the Prince. A light ripple of applause rose from the fascinated throng. Wellington, Britain's leading aficionado of the long game, made a noise like a wasp, for he knew, above all others present, that at this point of progression it would be a brave or foolish man who would risk the deployment of Jigg's Whip. Little did he know that such a man was in their midst.

'Turnpike Lane,' drawled Beau Nash, without dropping a stitch.

'Ole!' muttered the Iron Duke, and made a noise like another wasp.

'Earl's Court!' squealed the Prince, now quite beside himself, so everyone had to shove up a bit.

Garrick struck like a cobra. 'Perivale,' he spat.

'Earl's Court!' hooted the Prince, scarcely able to contain his belly.

Perspiration beaded the brow of the next in line, Viscount Bisquitz. 'Um…' he mumbled 'Tur…Tooting Bec?'

'Earl's Court!' howled the Prince, 'Gad's Trollies, gentlemen, am I not a pretty player at this sport? Or what?'

'Canning Town,' said the Vicar of Cliveden, slyly, for being a Master of Divinity he had the ecclesiastical 'back-doubles' off by heart, and well knew where this connection must lead. He little realised that he had been undone by his own ingenuity.

'I fear you find yourself in Mopsy, sir. Indeed you

do!' whispered Brummel, and the cleric's face went a
deathly white.

'Earl's Court!' boomed the Prince, waggling his legs
in the air to break, among other things, the tension.

'Now, Canning Town, I fancy,' smiled the cunning
Brummel.

'Earl's Court,' said Mad Jack.

A dreadful silence descended. Beau Nash dropped a
pin, and not a man present failed to hear it. The
silence seemed to last an eternity, although it probably
didn't. Every eye present swivelled wildly round the
room before alighting on Mad Jack. Jack brushed
them off impatiently, and stood his ground like a man,
which indeed he was.

'Earl's Court,' he repeated softly, with a voice full of
menace and a mouth full of peanuts. The Prince grew
visibly apoplectic.

'What?' he spluttered. 'What d'ye mean by it, sir?
Eh? Eh? What d'ye mean by it, I say? What d'ye mean,
I repeat?!' he repeated.

'I mean what I say, your Royal Highness,' replied
bold Jack, 'and what I say is Earl's Court sir, and that,
sir, is what I mean.'

'Ye cannot do this thus!' cried the Prince, a-wobble
with fury. 'Ye cannot do't, and there's an end on't!
Pah!'

The Prince's Chinese body servant, Pah, scurried to
his master's side and mopped his brow.

'Mop mine too,' gasped the Prince, and Pah obliged,
using the same handkerchief. Emotions in the room
now ran so high that none present noticed this folie
d'etiquette.

'Wellington, d'ye tell this upstart guttersnipe, Mad

Jack, that he stands in breach of manners, court protocol, and rules 17 and 98b of the game?'

'Indeed I will, Pah,' replied the Iron Duke, briefly astounded at the Chinaman's grasp of the finer points of the rule book; but before he could continue, up spoke Mad Jack himself, and addressed the Prince.

'You will forgive me for observing, sir,' he began, 'that,' he went on, 'it is customary for play to pass between the teams, each player present taking his turns in diagonal advancement against the clock. Yet you, sir, have been countering each and every move played with the Earl's Court Riposte. A fine and noble move in its place, I allow, but it pains me to note that your Royal Highness has been speaking out of turn.'

Another silence descended on the room, a silence even more silent than the one before. Beau Nash dropped three small buckets, but this time no one heard a sound. That's how silent it was.

'Mad by name, dead by breakfast!' growled Wellington to Turnip Townsend, who had turned green, and was sketching designs for an organic windmill. 'Do you hear a wasp, your Grace?' whispered Turnip.

Now, of course, the full and open-mouthed attention of the entire gathering was focussed closely on the Prince, who had turned Royal Blue, and appeared on the point of a seizure or, at best, a mishap in the linen department. It was hard to tell. Brummel was taking bets. At last the silence was broken.

'I say, you chaps!' spluttered the fat owl of the House of Hanover. 'We can't let the scoundrel get away with this!'

Mad Jack turned his level gaze on the Prince.

'I would go further, sir, and suggest, with all respect due to your station and your Royal Person, that you are little better than a selfish, cheating, dishonest barrel of grease, with no more idea of honesty and fair play than this penguin!' he cried, producing the bewildered bird with a flourish. A tentative smattering of applause greeted this startling coup d'oiseau.

'Dear God in Heaven!' wailed the Bishop of Bath and Wells, making a bolt for the door, in case some stranger should try to enter. Mad Jack, now well into his stride, strode up to Prince George and poked a finger into his voluminous chest area with a plodging sound that startled even the bats in the chimney.

'I go further yet, sir!' he went further, 'I put it to this here-gathered assemblage that His Royal Highness, the Blancmange of Hanover, is a big fat dirty chizzling cheat. With knobs on!'

The room erupted in a fury. Grown men waved their fists and said 'Boo'. It was a scene of uttermost chaos. Wigs writhed and shrank, beauty spots flew off powdered cheeks like bullets, cravats unfurled and shot across the room like comets. Smelling salts dropped from the ceiling on long tubes, and luggage came tumbling out of the overhead lockers.

'Gad's Plums!' ejaculated the Prince, struggling to adjust his life jacket, 'this is too much! Too much, d'ye mark me?'

Scandal! Up went the cry, and the gathering voted as if with one vote to demand satisfaction on behalf of their Royal companion. It was to be pistols at dawn.

Next morning, as the clocks struck dawn, the last wisps of mist lifted from the peak of Primrose Hill to

reveal His Royal Highness and some ten dozen of his
supporters shivering against the cold. Every man
present carried a horse pistol, primed, charged, and
with the safety catch not yet invented. They paced to
and fro, and then back again as they waited upon the
arrival of the man who had been so rash as to
question the salubricity of the Royal Person.

Noon fell, and still no sign of Jack. The men dined
off a sumptuous picnic provided by Mrs Fitzherbert,
laying aside their weapons as they lolled on the park
benches and tussocks of grass, delivered that morning
from Fortnum's, while the Prince demolished an entire
capon and spat out the pips as he reclined majestically
on Mrs Fitzherbert. Suddenly, the Duke of Wellington
sprang to his feet and clapped a spyglass to his eye.

'I spy with my little eye…' he began, and so the long
afternoon was spent in innocent sport, playing
conkers, and throwing each others' caps over the
hedge. As dusk began to fall they pitched camp, and
after posting sentries to their families at home, they all
prepared for the weary night, and all the other days
and nights of waiting that surely stretched ahead of
them. For all I know, they may be waiting there still.

As for Jack Camden, he was never seen again.

Not so mad, after all.

GREAT PLAYERS OF THE GAME
MOTHER ANNA OF WIDDICOMBE [15??–16??]

MYSTERY surrounds the early life of Mother Anna of Widdicombe, who was born in the late part of the early second half of the third quarter of the sixteenth century somewhere in the west of England. Legend has it she came from a well-to-do family who were amazed to the point of horror by her precocious antics. At the age of three she is reputed to have mastered the rudiments of Mornington Crescent, which she played incessantly with an imaginary friend whom she treated as the little brother she never had, much to the upset of the little brother she did have.

Records reveal that in 1567, at the age of perhaps eleven, she was taken to London's famous Harley Street to be examined by a child psychologist and then, when he couldn't help, by a grown-up one. The study of psychological disorders was in its infancy at that time, it being several centuries before Freud would formulate his theories of witty interruptions being at the root of human misery. Her examiner concluded she had been impregnated by the Devil, but when Anna explained she thought a more likely cause was penis fixation, her family disowned her and she was left to roam the streets of London.

It was then that she turned to the professional Mornington Crescent circuit, playing the game for money at fairs on market days alongside the cock-fighting rings, bear-baiting pits and dodgy hoop-la stalls. Her first recorded match took place at Stepney in the following spring when she beat a young chicken farmer from Wimbledon, Timothy the Hen Man, who went on to be beaten by every player in England during a short and much overrated career.

From that moment on, Anna never looked back and as a result was hit by a turnip cart as she crossed Blackfriars Bridge some months later. This appeared to upset the balance of her mind, just as it did the overloaded turnip cart. Times were hard for single women at the best of times, but especially so for one whose only skill lay in what was regarded as a solely male preserve.

She played on for another 40 years, and though her game skills never left her, and she lost not a single match in all that time, Mother Anna of Widdicombe's increasingly mad outbursts and rantings put fear into simple minds. She was eventually tried as a witch and sister of Satan. As she was punished by submersion in a small pond her last words were: 'Get me off this ducking stool' – or at least that is how they were reported at the time.

MORNINGTON CRESCENT
IN MUSIC AND LITERATURE

King Henry V rallies his troops.

Shakespeare's works present many allusions to
Mornington Crescent – for example, the first folio of
Henry V (not frequently performed):

'Once more unto the Bank, dear friends, once more;
And close Blackwall up with the Bridge of Red*.
In Hayes there's nothing so becomes East Ham
As Morden, Sheerness and good Beacontree;
But when Plaistow war blows in our ears,
Then imitate the Acton and the Ongar;
Saint Stephen to New Cross, summon up St John's Wood

---

*Redbridge

Disguise fair Leyton with Saint Saviour's stage;
O'er Hanger Lane and City, this confounded Hayes;
Southfields with Seven Dials and Weybridge Station.
Now set Blackheath and stretch the Vauxhall wide,
And teach them Kensington Gore and you good Homerton,
South Mimms, Cricklade, Kingsland, Forest Mere,
For St Mary's and Kew, East Cheam and Walton-on-
the-Naze
That hath not Holborn, Leicester Square and Guys.
I see on Strand like Houndsditch, Pinner and Whipps
Cross,
Hainault, Upham and St Barts. The game's afoot,
Follow your spirit, and be not rancorous;
Cry God for Hurlingham, Dingwall and St Pancorous!'

§ § § §

Nursery rhyme (sixteenth century) – unfinished:

One, two, Bakerloo
Three, four,

§ § § §

Popular travelling song (seventeenth century):

We all want to travel to Mornington Crescent,
For everyone tells us it's terribly pleasant,
And on the way home we shall dine on cold pheasant,
But nobody knows where it is.

An hilarious evening of music hall, Bexhill, 1987.

**Popular music-hall standard sung in theatres and pubs
the length and breadth of the country throughout 1887:**

I'm Lord Mornington Crescent,
I'm extremely unpleasant,
I dress up in ladies' attire;
Then leap from the closet
With a cry of 'How was it?'
And invariably pee in the fire.
I'm Cres! Cres!
In Mummy's own dress
I walk up Pall Mall night and day.
Almost everyone knows me,
A Cynthia or Rosemary
I'm Lord Mornington Crecent, hooray!

I'm Lord Mornington Crescent,
And all of you esn't,
I'm the last of the Bakerloo Line.
I've given up gels –
Well they say breeding tells
And it does, oh it does – so does wine.
I'm Cres! Cres!
A psychological mess,
My ambition's to appear on page three*
I sometimes get rather cross
I'm half the woman father was
I'm Lord Mornington Crescent, that's me!

𝇋 𝇋 𝇋 𝇋

Nursery rhyme (probably Victorian):

'O where have you been to, my fat little dog?'
  'To Mornington Crescent, by jig and by jog.'
'And what did you see there, my fat little pup?'
  'One stair that said "Down", and one stair that
said "Up".'
'O where have you been to, my fat little dog?'
  'To Mornington Crescent, by jig and by jog.'
'And what did you do there, my fat little pet?'
  'I went in the toilets, and got my ears wet.'
'O where have you been to, my fat little dog?'
  'To Mornington Crescent, by jig and by jog.'
'And will you go back there, my fat little friend?'
  'No thanks, it's incredibly boring.'
The End.

* Page three here refers not to The Sun but to page three of Hansard which,
in the 1920s, was trying to increase its readership in the House of Lords.

'Sleep Doggy Sleep' and 'Shamey Simla' [contemporary].
Transcript of the legendary Game played between the
two Rapsters during a Musical Entertainment at the
Komodo Klub, Streatham:

'Got to tell ya my opinion see ya dirty ho's mental, goin'
showin' her stuff down to Walthamstow Central.'

> *'Well diss you bitch ass rapper, got troubles my own,
> if ya hard call it Leyton Leyton Leytonstone.'*

'Yall act chikka chikka like ya never rap a bombin', like
you shake yo' snake over Clapham Common.'

> *'Ya want I open a can of whoop ass on you, makin'
> Bayswater, Goodge Street, and Ongar too.'*

'Word up! No washbag get me manning down, take ya
chances with the massive out of Canning Town.'

> *'Jibba jabba, jibba jabba!'*

'Jabba jibba, jabba jibba! Fool!'

> *'My name is? My name is? And my name is?'*

'Man I pity the fool puts up and mess with my scene,
gonna get right to it and eat Willesden Green.'

> *'Well I've enjoyed our chat, it's been remarkable
> pleasant, and it only remains to say "Mornington
> Crescent"!'*

'Wooooh Haa!!!'

Ω Ω Ω Ω

MORNINGTON CRESCENT FAQ

- What are the rules of Mornington Crescent?
- Can anyone explain the game of Mornington Crescent?
- Does Mornington Crescent have rules, and if so what are they?
- Where can I find the rules of Mornington Crescent?
- How does one play Mornington Crescent?
- What are the rules of Mornington Crescent?
- Will you please print the rules of Mornington Crescent?
- I have heard of a game called Mornington Crescent. What are the rules?
- Is Mornington Crescent a real game? If it is, does it have rules?
- My husband insists there are rules for Mornington Crescent. What are they?
- What are the rules of Mornington Crescent?
- What are the rules of Mornington Crescent?
- What are the rules of Mornington Crescent?
- Mornington Crescent: rules, please?
- What are the rules of Mornington Crescent?
- What is an FAQ?
  This is a frequently asked question, to which we have so far been unable to find the answer.

MORNINGTON CRESCENT
A HISTORY OF THE GAME

PART 3 **FROM THE NORMANS TO THE TIME OF CROMWELL**

THE first verifiable visual record of the game we call Mornington Crescent comes from the eleventh century and was found woven into the Bayeux Tapestry. Unfortunately, the section which depicts William Duc de Normandie playing a thrilling match against Humphroi de Pissoir et Douche-Complet in the 1066 finals of north-west Savoy (then one of the finest vintage cabbage production areas), was removed and inadvertently sold as a souvenir tea-towel in Hastings market.

After the Battle of Hastings, so called because it was fought at a place called 'Battle', the defeated English had Norman French foisted upon them. It was he who was commissioned to compile the Domesday Book, a record of all the interesting items found in the first Millennium Dome, then still open after sixty-six years in the hope of making a small profit. When, after several minutes, he ran out of things to write about, and not wishing to lose such a cushy and lucrative sinecure, Mr French extended the scope of the Domesday Book into a list of everything in England. Starting with London, he walked the streets of the city, which was then a small village with no shops, banks or post office, just like any small village in England today. As he walked, dictating location names to his scribe, he found the locals joining in, responding with other place names in a form of game. It was then that he realised that what he had witnessed being played only by the kings and courtiers of France was also popular in England. He had known it as 'Norman ton Crescent' (Norman, your Crescent) and this was how he intended it to be listed in the Domesday Book. However, his trusty servant scribe suffered from a rare disorder called 'Mnmismn' – the inability to tell the difference between the letters 'M' and 'N'. Having written down the game's name as 'Mornamtom Crescemt', the servant was sacked after lunch when Mr French asked him to butter his bun and stick a sausage in it.

Inevitably, 'Mornamtom Crescemt' became 'Mornhampton Cul de Sac', then 'Mooningto Crumpet' until eventually it was ignored completely, and everyone reverted to the English name of 'Mornington Crescent'. This was how it stayed until the time of Cromwell, probably.

The young Clement Freud appearing at a fancy-dress Mornington Crescent contest.

GREAT PLAYERS OF THE GAME
ETHAN JANKS [17??–1867]
The Idiot Savant of the Game

LITTLE is known of the early life of this humble son of the soil, who was to become one of the legendary 'instinctive' innovators of the Game. Born in the late eighteenth century, and believed by many (at least by his parents) to spring from simple farming stock, he began life as a labourer in the Hosiery Department of Tewkesbury's Shoppe. The hours were long, the work was arduous, and he was sustained by nothing more than a daily bowl of thin soup. The first authentic records of his career document his arrest and imprisonment for stealing a bread roll, a pat of butter, a plate and knife, a serviette, and cruet. He was sentenced to life imprisonment.

It was during his long years of confinement in the notorious 'Beachview' prison at Eastbourne that he was introduced to Mornington Crescent, a game eagerly played by the convicts as they sat picking oakum and waiting for their dressing gowns to dry. Janks, uneducated though he was, and unable to tell reading from writing, became remarkably adept at the Game, and his fame spread throughout the local community. He was in great demand at dinner parties, balls, and soirées, both inside and outside the prison, and it was at one of these that he slipped his manacles and made his escape.

After many sightings, his progress was eagerly followed by aficionados of the Game, as they saw a pattern beginning to emerge. Uckfield – Crawley – Dorking – Staines – Waterloo – Embankment – Goodge Street. He was arrested at Mornington Crescent. The sentence of life imprisonment was upgraded to deportment, and he was shipped to Mornington Island in the Gulf of Carpentaria off the northern coast of Queensland. Frail and old, a broken man, Ethan Janks eked out his declining years working as an occasional male model and running a hot-dingo stall. 'Coober Pedy', his Antipodean version of the Game, never took off, and during his brief tenure as Prime Minister of Australia, he died in obscurity.

BRUNEL: ONE MAN AND HIS TUNNEL
The Velvet Underground

The site offices at Rotherhithe were all of a flutter. The partners and staff of 'Maison Brunel' scampered hither and thither, flapping their hands, and uttering petulant squeals of annoyance. They skittered about with no apparent sense of purpose, for all the world like headless chickens, except that their heads were all more or less in place, and they were no chickens. Maps, charts, diagrams, and technical manuals had been pulled from the shelving, and lay festooned and scattered about the floor, yet at the heart of this storm of apparently purposeless activity there was a still small eye of calm.

Isambard Kingdom Brunel – played here by Peter Sallis.

Isambard Kingdom Brunel, the great man and founder of the firm, sat deep in thought on his unusually high stool at the highest drawing-table ever built. His was a small but imposing figure. He sat four foot three in his stout steel-toed leather boots, rough suit of off-black hessian, voleskin weskit, and high-collared shirt of cleanest white taffeta, set off with a coal-black cravat of finest Chantilly canvas, all of which were concealed beneath a voluminous 'Japonais' housecoat of heliotrope silk, ornamented with a traditional design of sparrows catching spiders among the plum blossoms. Upon his head he sported a black stove-pipe hat of lacquered aluminium, both shiny and tall (five and a half foot high if it was an inch), stamped discreetly on the brim with the 'IKB' logo in burnished bronze. It was the house style.

The differently-tall genius stared hard at the paper before him. He was designing a new tunnel to pass beneath the River Thames, and indeed most of London, running straight as a die (or any other six-sided shape) from A to B (to be confirmed). So far he had drawn an elliptical oval, shaped like an egg standing on one end, which he had meticulously labelled 'Hole in the Ground'. From the top and bottom of this figure he had ruled two parallel straight lines, and written 'Tunnel' in the space between them. Now the problem that exercised his mind was how to finish off the other end. Something lacy in latticework perhaps? No, too 1836. A simple cuff? An ornate cuff? Should he risk a Raglan? Or perhaps the dimensions could blossom into a wide 'leg-of-mutton' shape leading to…leading to what? He scratched his head with his pen, then scribbled a quick calculation with his comb. Of course! The most obvious idea was always the best. He rapidly delineated a matching oval shape at the far end of the tunnel, and labelled it 'Hole in the Ground – 2'.

'Finished!' he cried in triumph.

'Oh thank Heaven for that!' exclaimed George Wimpey, his right-hand man, 'Here was me fretting myself to death!' He fanned himself with a copy of *Engineer's Realm* and dabbed Eau-de-Cologne behind each of his beautifully manicured ears. 'Did you hear that, Ove? Issy's done it again!'

'I know, I heard!' chirped Arup, throwing a lever on the pocket steam engine in the corner, which spluttered into life. Brunel grabbed the iron hook, and connected it to his watch chain, then swung off his high stool as the jib of the derrick, powered by the engine, swung him across the room, landing him precisely on the mantelpiece. A few minor adjustments, and he was standing on the hearth-rug, displaying his plan for the tunnel.

'Look at this!' trilled Wimpey, summoning Costain from the breakfast nook, where he was reviving his strength with a cup of lemon-violet and rosemint tea after his morning's exertions arranging girders on site. 'Ooooh! Clever girl!' he fluted with raised eyebrows, as he gave Brunel a saucy tweak, then skipped playfully across the cluttered room and hid behind an old ship's boiler.

Little Taylor Woodrow, the office lad, bustled in with the mid-morning tray of pina coladas, followed by McAlpine, the bullet-headed foreman, who strode into the room, black leather trousers squeaking manfully. Dark glasses and a full black moustache gave his features an air of manly mastery and mystery, and the tattoos of gearing mechanisms, suspension coupling devices, and load-bearing stretch-steelwork rippled on his muscular arms. A fine sheen of sweat covered his exposed torso, a thin streak of rust tracing its way down from his iron bellybutton-ring, for he had spent a strenuous morning at the half-completed engine shed at Paddington, selecting the colours for the rivets.

'I brought ye the publicity stills from the photo shoot, hen,' he announced, throwing aside his peaked leather cap, and flinging the contents of a large packet on the table. Chief Engineer Wimpey registered his delight, then flicked rapidly through the prints, uttering little noises of approval as he examined the pictures.

'Ooh, here's a divine one of you, Issy. Love the chains!'

Brunel brushed the photographs impatiently aside, and laid out his plan for the tunnel. He pointed out the finer details with his folding ivory-handled pre-stressed Toledo steel pointing thing:

'Observe gentlemen, the London Tunnel. This will be the centrepiece of our Spring Collection!'

'Oh, it's gorgeous, Issy!' exclaimed Arup, 'I honestly swear this is your best work since the Clifton Suspension Bridge!'

At the mention of the sacred name, a reverent hush fell on the assembly, broken only by the clanking as they removed their hats. The Clifton Suspension Bridge! Brunel's undisputed masterpiece, a towering pinnacle of engineering, unmatched until a hundred years later, when Howard Hughes was to adapt its design for the 'Brassière', an ill-fated flying boat. The respectful silence was shattered by Brunel replacing his hat.

'Come, gentlemen,' he instructed, 'let us address this tunnel! And what a tunnel it will be! A tunnel like no other!'

His audience stood agog.

'This, my friends, will be the world's first tunnel that is fully upholstered.' A communal gasp greeted these words. 'Yes, upholstered!' he continued, 'End to end, wall to wall, tip to top. In Plum Velvet, I fancy…'

'With buttons!' exclaimed Costain.

'And tassels!' added the excited Arup, hopping up and down.

'And gilt frogging around the vents!' piped young Taylor Woodrow. Brunel smiled indulgently, and ruffled the lad's ginger mop, then passed it round so that everyone else could have a good ruffle at it too.

Wimpey, picturing the Master's proposed marvel of engineering in his mind's eye, clasped his hands with awe. 'The House of Telford will be green with envy!' he whispered.

'Aye, as long as the French dinna beat us to it,' growled McAlpine.

'I have no fears from that quarter,' said Brunel, 'M. Eiffel is a mere sensationaliste. I'll warrant you'll never see his designs copied in the High Street. Now, to business. I am minded to begin our tunnel at Greenwich.'

'Greenwich!' exclaimed Wimpey, 'That's brilliant! No fear of over-crowding in this tunnel!'

'Aye, Greenwich is all very well and good,' rumbled McAlpine, 'but what aboot the other end? Where does the damn thing come oot?'

'Hmm. Where to dig "Hole in the Ground – 2"?' mused Brunel, stroking his chin (which the diminutive engineer only just managed to reach). 'Any ideas, Wimpey?'

'Hackney Marshes! Plenty of good digging to be had in Hackney Marshes!'

'Pah!' grunted McAlpine, 'Allumial Quadrupary Cretinaceous Clay. Unstable, heavy as sin, and water-logged to boot. Did you no read the article in this week's Gentleman's Digging Digest?'

'Why don't we…' faltered Taylor Woodrow, 'er…that is to say, why don't you make use of a hole somewhere that has already been dug?'

Everyone exchanged glances, then focussed uncertainly on Brunel.

'I like your thinking, young 'un!' chuckled the great man. 'Come along boys, put your brains to the grindstone! Where do we find the hole we need?'

'Piccadilly Circus!' yodelled Costain, flouncing about more than was strictly necessary. 'There is the most fan-tas-tic hole slap-ding-dong right in the middle of it! I put it there myself. Cast-iron lattice shell, steel and timber bulwarks with bronze ribbing and quarter-inch lightweight plating. And all sunk a full one hundred feet below ground!'

'It wasnae meant to sink, though, was it?' muttered McAlpine darkly, 'It was supposed to be a Zeppelin!' Costain blushed and stared at his peep-toe galoshes. It was true, in a sense it had been his fault, but he had never since purchased an altimeter from Gieves and Hawkes.

'Blackfriars?' suggested Arup. 'It already has a

handy little tunnel quite close by. You know, that one I put in years ago. It's never been used…'

Wimpey snorted. 'Well, of course it hasn't! I mean, who wants to use a tunnel that wobbles in the wind?'

'You bitch!' screamed Arup. 'Once! It wobbled once, during the Grand Opening. And it only wobbled then because the Queen and Prince Albert were larking about!'

'Willesden Junction,' said McAlpine firmly, surveying himself in the mirror, and rejecting a Native American Headdress in favour of a Hard Hat.

'You can't invoke DuValier's tangent,' sighed Brunel, 'not from Ironmongers Triangle.'

'I was advancing by Caledonian Mid-Phase Drift, which I trust you find no fault with!' countered the dour Scot, planting his weatherbeaten hands on a pair of gnarled hips.

'Get your hands off my hips!' giggled Costain.

'Think again, Issy,' continued McAlpine coolly.

'Very well,' shrugged Brunel. 'You leave me little choice but Whitechapel.'

'Grant's coupling? I think not, Guv'nor!' chided Wimpey. 'It's got to be Highgate.'

Brunel glared at his Chief Engineer, and in that moment's silence little Taylor Woodrow, who had been hopping from foot to foot in his eagerness to join in, sang out in a clear high treble:
'Mornington Crescent!'

The atmosphere became electrified. It was as if the room had been dazzled by a flash of lightning, and now they were counting the seconds until the thunder. The thunder never came. Without a word, Brunel strode to the Pneumatic Chute and climbed inside, shutting the hatch behind him. Through the toughened glass his hand could be seen reaching for the valve control, then with a soft 'Ploof!' he was gone, sucked into the long tube and shooting off to his secret lair in Birkenhead. The partners and staff of 'Maison Brunel' looked at one another, then turned their gaze on the bewildered Taylor Woodrow, who stood shaking and close to tears.

'Don't blame yourself, son,' said McAlpine, gruffly, 'You weren't to know.'

'It's just that we never mention that name in the Master's presence,' explained Costain, 'Never!'

'It's a long story,' said Wimpey, perching himself on a pile of railway sleepers and settling among the cushions, 'But I dare say you have the right to hear it now.' He lit a clay pipe of tobacco, fixed it into a long ebony clay-pipe holder, and began his yarn.

'It was Mr Brunel's very first solo commission, many years ago. He thought it would make his name – to construct the first ever underground railway station in the world. He set out to make it the biggest, grandest, most beautiful underground station mankind would ever see. And, if it hadn't been for desperate bad luck and a cruel quirk of fate, so it would have been; I know, because I've seen the plans. Over a mile in length, nearly half a mile wide, Mornington Crescent had everything. The lot! The very latest Double-Case O'Shaughnessy alloy casing plates, wrought-iron stanchions, hand-cast rivets, six balanced Pratt and Whitney steam turbines, four funnels, six masts, and a bandstand. The cantilevered suspension system was an innovation, and the dining room had a dance-floor big enough to accommodate the Ballet Russe.

Passengers could stroll along leafy boulevards between the automatic water-driven ticket machines and the Kinematoscope Lounge or the Menagerie. And all this below ground, mark you! Imagine! There were eighteen great hydraulic lifts that hauled the passengers the 200 feet up to ground level, where they could get on the trains. Those same eighteen great hydraulic lifts would then carry disembarking passengers down to the station level, where they could wait for one of the eighteen great hydraulic lifts to carry them up the 200 feet to the street exit. I tell you, sweetie, it was magnificent!'

'But it was cursed!' rumbled McAlpine.

'But it was cursed (thank you, Mac)!' continued Wimpey, testily. 'There were strange goings-on. Issy's foreman, the great Jesse, told him the workmen were growing uneasy.'

'They fell behind with the work,' twittered Arup. 'Well, you know workmen! And then the money ran out, the deadline date for completion came and went, the sponsors, Lyons Corner House, refused any further funding, and the whole project ground to a halt. Well, it was still only half finished! They hadn't even plumbed in the ladies' toilet pedestal, though God knows what the problem could have been, seeing as there was only the one. I mean, you'd have thought, wouldn't you…?'

'So whatever did Mr Brunel do?' asked Taylor Woodrow, sitting down on an upturned silver-plated bilge-pump.

'What only a man like I. K. Brunel would even think of doing!' said Wimpey, with a gleam in his eye. 'He determined to finish the job on his own. Day and night he laboured in the pitch dark with only the glow from a hand-held chandelier to light his way. And the work took its toll. On one occasion he almost lost his life!'

'There was never an iceberg!' scoffed McAlpine, chewing on a plug of Sailor-boy Shag tobacco. 'The man was seeing things.'

'Maybe, maybe not,' went on Wimpey, 'But when Issy first went down there he was a strapping six-footer in robust good health. When he came out he was a white-haired gibbering tiddler. Before the workmen left, they had complained of strange noises: banging sounds like someone knocking from behind the wall panelling. Well, alone in the dark, the Guv'nor heard those noises too. They almost drove him mad! One night in a frenzy he set to tearing out the panels with his bare teeth, and to his horror he found, dear God, do you know what he found?'

McAlpine leaned towards the shivering youngster and thrust his face close to his.

'He found that two of his welders had been walled in…alive!' he hissed.

'Yes, all right, no need to frighten the boy,' said Wimpey, impatiently. 'True, the men had been walled in, but luckily for them they'd been sealed into one of the first class cabins, with running water and a walk-in cold store. When they were bored they used to climb out of the porthole and scrape their way to the surface, then go and pick up girls at the Trocadero. When Issy found them they were having a party.'

'That's what finished him, poor man,' said Costain, handing round a plate of Gypsy Creams. 'Oh, in time he recovered, and did quite well for himself actually;

but he never worked on Mornington Crescent again.'

'But the station…' said Taylor Woodrow.

'There is no station,' explained Wimpey. 'The underground line runs through it now, but no trains stop there. What the passengers see as they pass is a cardboard and papier-mâché mock-up. The whole business was hushed up, you see. Oh, there's talk of building a real station of more modest proportions on the site, but I doubt we'll see it in our lifetime.'

'And that,' said Wimpey in a voice like doom, 'is why that name has never been uttered in the Master's presence from that day…to this!'

For a moment, the company sat in solemn silence.

Whey-faced and trembling, the shaken office lad rose unsteadily and left the room. As the door closed behind him, the hatch to the Pneumatic Chute flew open, and Brunel hopped out.

'Ha ha ha!' he guffawed, 'I can't believe the little chap fell for it! Ho ho ho!'

The partners and staff of 'Maison Brunel' shrieked with laughter, and slapped each other's thighs.

'Aah…' said McAlpine, 'Bless!'

શ્ર   શ્ર   શ્ર   શ્ર

A GUIDE TO MORNINGTON CRESCENT WEBSITES
(IN ORDER OF USEFULNESS)

http://www.playmorningtoncrescent.co.uk/start.php
An exhilarating if primitive opportunity to play Tim
Brooke-Taylor, Barry Cryer or Graeme Garden online.
Beginners are advised to start with Tim.

http://madeira.physiol.ucl.ac.uk/people/jim/mc_em.html
The Encyclopaedia Morningtonia. Much more than
you could ever wish to know.

http://www.netcomuk.co.uk/~mrw/isihac/mcvari.html
Comprehensive summary of recent Mornington
Crescent variations as heard on Radio 4's *I'm Sorry I
Haven't A Clue*.

http://www.londontransport.co.uk/tube/index.shtml
Just click 'maps' for a comprehensive diagram of the
area of play. Users with the benefit of a printer might
wish to produce for themselves a free board.

http://metadyne.tripod.com/MCT-reopen.html
A celebration of the 1998 reopening of the famous
tube station in words and pictures.

http://www.cix.co.uk/~gil/data/morn.htm
Spoof history and description of the rules to
Mornington Crescent. Entertaining nonsense.

Mornington Crescent Newsgroups:
These provide an opportunity to chat online with
players throughout the world. Try
alt.games.mornington.crescent or
uk.games.mornington-crescent

GREAT PLAYERS OF THE GAME
LORD KNARESBOROUGH (1740–1815)
The Yorkshire Rake

HUGH de Montague Smythe-D'Arrison-Smythe, later Lord Knaresborough, is regarded by many as among the finest amateur players of the modern game. Gambler, explorer, poet, serial adulterer and landscape gardener, Smythe-D'Arrison-Smythe (or 'Flash Hughie' as he was known) was blessed with a mane of golden hair, eyes of translucent blue and fingers of rich bottle green.

Even today, rumours of his sexual exploits still abound. Can he really have bedded seven women between Knightsbridge and Piccadilly Circus in a three-stage manoeuvre played to Morton's 1st stratagem (and two of them while executing a deft backward triangulation)? Too right he could. Each one of his conquests was left disarmed, entranced and slightly flushed about the bosom. There was no getting away from it; in those elegant, soil-stained hands, the game was pure unalloyed sex. 'And,' to quote *Debrett's*, 'boy could he play!'

At Eton he won the Babbington Trophy (for Excellence in the Game) five years in a row, an achievement made all the more remarkable by the fact that he was only at the school for two terms, due to a misunderstanding over Matron's schedule. At 19 he picked up the Junior Mornington trophy after winning in three straight moves, and by 22 he had defeated Sir Nicholas Busby himself, official MC player to the Court of King George III. He soon came to the notice of the King himself, and might well have benefited from the relationship, had he not insisted on correcting King George's dislike of the garden 'ditch'; the King adjudged Smythe-D'Arrison-Smythe's exclamations of 'ha-ha!' disrespectful in the extreme, and he received no further contact with the Palace.

On inheriting the title of Lord Knaresborough after the death of his uncle (whose admiration for his talented nephew was such that he was only too pleased to disinherit his eldest son and rightful heir in his favour), Smythe-D'Arrison-Smythe wasted no time in introducing the game to the staff and tenants of his Yorkshire estate – with a few variations of his own. To his primitive neighbours he must have seemed like an exotic butterfly, no doubt due to the theatrical moth costume he wore day and night. In fact, so popular was he with the local womenfolk that together they managed to reinstate their new landlord's medieval *droit de Seigneur*, despite strong protestations from the Church.

Smythe-D'Arrison-Smythe died outside what is now the entrance to Camden Town underground station while attempting to demonstrate the Perfect Looped-Shift by performing an illegal U-turn. He was struck by a hackney carriage bound for Mornington Crescent under Phelps' 2nd Protocol.

MORNINGTON CRESCENT
A HISTORY OF THE GAME
PART 4 **THE MODERN AGE**

The Modern Age of Mornington Crescent is generally accepted to have begun as recently as 1543. In that year, Copernicus published his revolutionary theory that the Circle Line travels around the sun, and not the other way round. Half the trains on the Circle Line do, of course, travel the other way round, but Copernicus was right in theory, apart from this fact. His mistake is understandable, since in his day there were no trains on the Central Line, nor was there a Central Line as such: Copernicus was simply putting forward his point of view as a theoretical Astro-Physicist, there being no real Astro-Physicists around at the time. The Copernican rules were promoted by the Italian Galileo/Galilei, and the game enjoyed a new lease of life. In Britain 'Real' Mornington Crescent was played indoors for the first time at Hampton Court [which can be found on O'Grady's parallel, two clicks beyond Hounslow West].

Years passed, which came as no surprise to Sir Isaac Newton, famed for having an apple fall on his head as he was burning his fingers pulling a piece of pig meat out of a camp fire, leading to the discovery of Roast Pork, Apple Sauce, and his theory of Gravy. Newton was briefly interested in the game, and although he was never a great player, future generations have been grateful for his laws of motion, which paved the way for the scientific game. Mass, momentum, velocity, and inertia are now an essential part of any Grand

Master's arsenal, and without them no-one would even dare to attempt Flamsteed's Torque.

Samuel Pepys records in his diary that he had the Lytteltons round for a fish supper, and that his guests introduced him to 'the genteel game of Moaning Tom Cheshunt'. It is not clear whether or not this was a variation of the Great Game itself, and after the bottle-spinning round, Pepys's account of the evening's entertainment becomes a little cryptic.

Nevertheless the game spread throughout the world, largely thanks to the efforts of intrepid explorers like Mungo Park and his sister Belsize. Many great names in the worlds of Art, Literature, Science, and Politics have been associated with the game over the years, and incidentally it should be noted that G. K. Chesterton, novelist, poet, philosopher, polemicist, and wit, who contributed so much to the advancement of social theory, and was a vigorous spokesman for Roman Catholic orthodoxy, was quite fat.

Strangely, Mornington Crescent never really took off in Guatemala.

Automation introduced at Mornington Crematorium.

THE HUMPHREY LYTTELTON INTERVIEW

Humph present at 'The Birth Of The Blues' antenatal class.

Richard Dimbleby's award-winning interview with Humphrey Lyttelton, recorded just hours before Mr Lyttelton's legendary 1951 World Amateurs Final in Helsinki against Heinz Kipf.

(Reproduced in full)

Dimbleby: 'What was it that first interested you in the game?'

Lyttelton: 'As a child I remember that time of evening when we small folk would be sent to the nursery while the grown-ups took a turn at the "Game of Games", which is how they mysteriously referred to it. We would sit on the stairs, peeping through the banisters, listening to the howls of merriment. Then one night my uncle Bruce came out of the bedroom, and chased us back down to the nursery. From that moment on, I was hooked.'

Dimbleby: 'Was the game played with any success at your old school, Eton?'

Lyttelton: 'Only the Flashers [prefects] and other senior members of Spud were allowed to play. That was because the juniors weren't permitted to wear waistcoats. We were forbidden to play for money, of course, so we played for fags. I remember one evening when Lady Luck was positively beaming on me, and when all the available fags had run out, Disraeli minor had to bet with a promissory note to the value of 100 fags from Winchester. I have that note to this day, just in case.'

Dimbleby: 'We all know how the game kept up morale during the war. German morale, mainly. Do you recall any amusing incidents involving the game during your wartime experience?'

Lyttelton: 'I remember D-Day was postponed for 48 hours to allow Montgomery and Eisenhower to finish their game to decide who would be Supreme Allied Commander. Which was good, otherwise D-Day would have been called B-Day, causing much hilarity to the French.'

Dimbleby: 'In view of some of the more unfortunate incidents during the early stages of competition, would you be in favour of a more formal process of drug testing?'

Lyttelton: 'Certainly the drugs should be properly tested before we take them.'

Dimbleby: 'I understand you come from a Mornington Crescent playing family. Do you know which of your ancestors first displayed any proficiency at the game?'

Lyttelton: 'The Lytteltons are actually the cadet branch of the Byggeton family, so I may well be descended from Big "Byggie" Byggeton, the legendary Big Giant of Euston. In the Middle Ages it's said he would prevent travellers from reaching Mornington Crescent by clouting them with his oaken club and stealing their oatcakes. Then there's Captain Horatio "Tug" Lyttelton, who sailed into Marseilles harbour, set fire to the boatyard, sank three French ships, and beat the French Commander in a Tricorn game of Mornington Croissant before they overpowered him. He's my nephew.'

The scoreboard at the World Finals in 1951.

Dimbleby: 'It was rather touching to see this year's championships opened by a child – six-year-old Timothy Brooke-Taylor of Buxton. Viewers will have seen you exchanging words with him at the end of the ceremony. Can you remember what you said to him that should have reduced him to tears in that way?'

Lyttelton: 'I told Timothy I saw a great future for him playing the game for 28 years or more on a light-hearted BBC wireless programme. It's a pity the boy didn't get the joke, but then I don't suppose jokes will be his thing either.'

Dimbleby: 'Your rise through the game can only be described as prolific. How do you find the time to relax and pursue your hobbies?'

Lyttelton: 'Pursuing hobbies is anything but relaxing, I can assure you. They are among the rarest and swiftest of our native birds of prey.'

Dimbleby: 'This brings me to my next question. I'm told you're a keen orthinologist?'

Lyttelton: 'Not so much an orthinologist, more a word botcher.'

Dimbleby: 'Do you adopt any special dietary regimes when approaching a major competition such as this?'

Lyttelton: 'Baked beans, sprouts, cabbage, and Jerusalem artichokes can lend a somewhat antisocial atmosphere to the game, which is unfair on one's opponents, so I have lashings of them with my bubble and squeak before a match.'

Dimbleby: 'Many former Mornington Crescent champions go on to work as referees on the amateur circuit. Is this something you think might appeal to you in the future?'

Lyttelton: 'We don't have referees. The adjudicator is called the chairman. Frankly, it doesn't appeal to me – it's a thankless task open only to over-the-hill, talentless, egotistical failures who gain nothing but abuse from both players and audience alike. Goodness, I'd almost be better off taking up the trumpet.'

Dimbleby: 'Your extraordinary comeback in that quarter-final match with Benjamin Zloti of Israel was thrilling to watch. What was going through your mind when he called "Regents Park" on the diagonal?'

Lyttelton: 'To be quite honest I was rattled. He was, after all, only one stamp away from a seven-letter station. Luckily the bubble and squeak kicked in at the crucial moment.'

Dimbleby: 'Many viewers have telephoned to say how impressed they are with your all-round game. Do you have any favourite moves?'

Lyttelton: 'Yes. The famous double pincer movement to Clapham and Turnham Green.'

Sarcastic graffiti artist caught on film.

THE ARTFUL DODGSON
A dark episode in the annals of the Game

Charles Dickens sat alone at his writing desk in gloomy thought. The quill pen hung motionless in his leaden fingers, the surface of the ink in his inkwell as slick and smooth and untroubled as the surface of a mill pond full of ink. His imagination lay as heavy and solid and indigestible in his mind as an undigested suet pudding in his mind would have lain. Today Inspiration was a stranger to him, just as it had been a stranger these three days past, and truth be told, for a full month before that, or to be more accurate, as it had been for almost the whole of the year. As usual, it was nearly Christmas. Dickens hadn't written a novel since *Our Mutual Friend*, which he had knocked out on a rainy Saturday afternoon in early February, when the football had been cancelled. Now, in the drawer to his left, lay his unfinished novel: *The Mystery of Edwin Drood*. In the empty drawer to his right lay his unstarted novel: *Malachi Wizziwig's Mandolin*. Even his drawers mocked him.

Rising from his desk, Dickens crossed to the window and stared out. It looked like snow. It fell in flakes, which settled on the roofs and cobblestones, and it was white. Yes, it was snow all right. He sighed. For the hundredth time, he forced himself to face the fact: he simply couldn't write any more. Two days ago he had tried to write a shopping list, but had been forced to give up halfway through Chapter Two. What a state for the great man to be in.

Dickens crossed to the piano, where he let his fingers wander idly over the keys, while he went downstairs for a glass of milk. He returned almost at once, in an ill temper and un-refreshed. The cow had been empty. Normally his cleaning lady, Mrs Twerp, brought a bunch of grass every morning to refill the beast, but he now remembered that he had given her the day off to go to some poor child's funeral. In a moment of kindly thought, he hoped that she had been lucky enough to find one. He sighed. It was at times like this that he wished he too had a hobby.

Once more that familiar feeling rose within the author's bosom. Dickens was irked. What irked him, however, was not the desertion of his muse. No, what irked him was the sure and certain knowledge that he knew the man responsible, the author of his predicament, the very engine of his downfall.

'Carroll!' he growled venomously. 'Lewis bloody Carroll!'

Dickens curled up in his favourite armchair and began to brood. 'Lewis Carroll' indeed! It wasn't even his real name. That was Charles Lutwidge Dodgson, and Dickens never trusted a man who wrote under a false name (conveniently forgetting that he himself had been christened 'Marion Spangler Dickens'). For many a long year, Dickens had been the Lion, the King, the Giant of English Letters. His position had been undisputed, until this upstart polymath Dodgson had wafted on to the scene. Already he was the talk of Bloomsbury Square, Fitzroy Square, and other literary circles. They worshipped him as once they had worshipped Dickens. And for what? The man had only written two little books, and both of them were absolute nonsense. Dickens had written loads of books! And damned big ones, at that! Dickens wrote literature, Dodgson just made up the words as he went along. Oh how fearfully clever! Yes, that's why they all idolised him, he was so clever. Dodgson, the Oxford Scholar, distinguished mathematician, noted photographer with his studies of young girls in their native state of innocence, completely devoid of lust-engendering clothing, strangers to the alluring waist-nipper corset, the sensuous bustier, and the maddeningly erotic bustle…

Dickens paused in his brooding while he wiped his chin, and at that very moment was struck by a thought. Might there not be a way to dislodge his rival in the public's affection, and reclaim his rightful place? Some form of public humiliation, perhaps? That was it! Dickens knew that Dodgson had a weakness for word-play and games; he could never resist a challenge. 'That will be his undoing!' thought Dickens to himself, as a plan began to hatch in his head.

Christmas Eve. The Clerkenwell Temperance Hall and Top Hat Warehouse was packed to the point of bursting by devoted followers of the great 'Lewis Carroll'. Steam rose from the eager audience, some of whom were forced to stand on each other's heads, and some less fortunate had to stand on their own, while urchins clung to the beams, and stout widows perched on the picture rail. Pedlars forced their way among the throng, selling hot chestnuts, tangerines, nuts, geese and Christmas puddings. An old organ-grinder was ejected for causing a public nuisance. On the platform, 'Lewis Carroll' was reciting 'Jabberwocky'.

In the shadows at the back of the hall, Dickens winced and grunted. More confounded made-up words! As Dodgson finished his recitation, Dickens realised that the writer had accidentally read out the first verse again instead of the last one, but the audience didn't notice. They clapped and cheered him to the echo! Dickens stepped forward into the light. As the tumult faded, he spoke out in ringing tones:

'Bethnal Green!'

Dodgson regarded the intruder with a gaze like ice.

'Ah, I perceive we have a celebrity in our midst,' he murmured.

'I say again, sir, Bethnal Green!' repeated Dickens, in a voice like ice.

'I heard you, sir,' said Dodgson, with ears like ice.

'Then what have you to say, sir?' asked Dickens, pointing a finger like ice.

'Shall I say…Aldgate East?' ventured Dodgson, with a nose like ice.

'Indeed you shall, sir,' cried Dickens, adjusting his trousers against the sudden cold, 'For I shall say Finsbury Park!'

The crowd caught its breath, then roared its admiration for this masterstroke. What rapture! Dodgson had fallen into the trap. Dickens watched with quiet satisfaction as he saw the man falter. He could see that the Nonsense-Monger, working rapidly through the next eighteen moves in his head, had realised at once that he was bound to lose – one more move, and he would be on his way to Nip, opening every one of O'Callaghan's Loops and Bounding

Channels behind him as he went.

'Very ingenious, Mr Dickens,' whispered Dodgson, stroking the white cat he always carried with him, just in case.

'Ha ha!' exclaimed Dickens, dramatically. 'Ha ha!' he repeated, even more dramatically. 'Ha ha!' he went again, which sort of worked, but might have been a mistake. And then he was gone – through the jubilant jostling throng, out of the door and into the street, and the fresh cold air and swirling snow. How pretty the world suddenly seemed!

He walked. He walked and walked, dizzy with triumph. On and on he walked, turning left or right on a whim. He walked in all directions. How far he walked he did not know, but at length he rested, leaning against a sign which read 'Clerkenwell Temperance Hall and Top Hat Warehouse – 107 yds'. In a doorway opposite, an old blind beggar was scraping out the tune of a festive carol on a table leg which he had bought from a man who had told him it was a violin. Dickens crossed to him, and threw a golden guinea into his hat.

'Merry Christmas, old man!' beamed Dickens with a heart full of good cheer. 'A very Merry Christmas!'

The old beggar touched his forelock in grateful disbelief. 'Cockfosters!' he chortled.

Dickens walked on, whistling merrily, but after three paces he stopped, and turned. Turned to see the beggar cast aside his smoked glasses, his filthy rags, and his table leg to stand revealed. Dickens' legs turned to jelly, his stomach turned to custard, his head to whipped cream. Anyone could see he was a trifle upset. More, he was dashed!

'Dodgson!' he gulped. Dear Heaven, the fiend was a master of disguise as well! In desperation he stammered 'Gur…gur…gur…Goodge Street!' It wasn't a Terminal Banker, but as a Holding Conjunction it would suffice. With a contemptuous laugh, the 'beggar' sprinted up a dark alley, and vanished from sight. Dickens needed time to think. His enemy had found the one chink in his plan, by deploying the arcane Crowley's Pentagram Manoeuvre. With mind reeling, he staggered into the night, through the slums and stews, past so-called 'thieves' kitchens', where they charged outrageous prices for a mouthful of beef with a tiny carrot in a strawberry coulis. At last he saw the lighted windows of an honest public house, and decided that he would think more clearly after a mutton chop and a pint of porter, but as he drew closer he heard the merry crowd inside singing 'Twinkle twinkle, little bat'. Disgusted, he turned on his heel, only to find his path blocked by a tiny pale-faced orphan hobbling towards him with the aid of a wooden crutch.

'Merry Christmas, kind gentleman,' quavered the wretched child, 'God bless us every…'

'Shut up!' cried Dickens. 'Where the devil am I?'

'Turnham Green!' crowed the waif with malevolent glee. Dodgson!

'Eek! Tottenham Hale!' squealed Dickens. It was a desperate Scattershot Defensive Reflex, but it would cover his Rear Approaches for the moment. Furiously he seized the orphan's crutch, and raised it to poke him in the eye. A heavy hand fell on his shoulder, and a stern voice rang out.

Dickens turned to see a stout police sergeant.

'And what might you be a-doing of and no mistake?' enquired the stony-faced limb of the law.

'I was going to injure this orphan, officer,' explained the Great Writer, in a reasonable tone.

'Ho yus?' said the copper. 'And what orphan might that be? Stepney Green!'

'What?'

Dickens whirled round. The orphan was there no longer. He whirled back. The Sergeant was nowhere to be seen.

'Clapham Common!' he yelled to the empty air. Then, horrified, he realised his terrible mistake.

He ran. How he ran! He put one foot in front of the other as fast as he could, that's how he ran! In no time at all he found himself outside his lodgings.

Dickens bolted the front door behind him, bolted up the stairs to his room, and bolted half a packet of Bath Olivers to calm his nerves. The dishevelled author was gasping for breath, and cascades of sweat poured down his back, becoming twin cataracts that thundered down the back of his legs and formed a small but attractive lagoon on the linoleum. Alone at last! Sanctuary! He took a deep breath, and briskly re-shevelled himself in front of the glass. But what was that? Had he heard a foot fall on the stairs? Yes! And by the sound of it, the foot had fallen all the way from top to bottom. He heard a volley of muffled curses, and then the sound of feet, once more climbing slowly towards his chamber. He armed himself with a rolled-up copy of *Barnaby Rudge*, checked that it was loaded, and took a position behind the door, which was already beginning to creak open…

Into the room shuffled a generously whiskered and

aromatic old crone: his cleaning lady, Mrs Twerp.

'Ah there you are, Mister Charley-boy. I brought you some wittles, Lord ha' mussy! Ho ho, 'tis naught but a glass of milk and a plate of brawn. Tee hee! He was a rare man for his wittles, was Mr Twerp, and I do not dissemble, sir. "All puppies at ninepence!" Nay, a rare man for his wittles, that he was.'

With that she flung her apron over her face and began weeping heartily, violently shaking the wedding cake she always carried until the mice squealed, as all the while her feet traced a silent gavotte across the hearth-rug.

'Dear God!' muttered Dickens to himself, 'And they ask me where I get my ideas from!'

It was apparent that the funeral Mrs Twerp had attended had been a roaring success. Her hat had been knocked askew, her clothes still held a few pieces of black confetti, and peeping out of her pocket was a pink fluffy monkey she must have won at the hoop-la stall. Judging by its presence around her neck, she had clearly caught the wreath. And yet, as Dickens took in these details, there was something about Mrs Twerp that was somehow…different. His face darkened as the realisation formed in his mind.

'Dodgson!' he hissed through clenched teeth. Then, replacing the clenched teeth on the mantelpiece, he dealt 'Mrs Twerp' a tremendous blow behind the ear with the rolled-up book. The body fell like a stone. Dickens, like a man possessed, attacked the motionless form with the toasting fork, then pausing only to apply a simple garrotte fashioned from the bell pull, he threw the limp figure into a barrel of tar he always kept to hand, and set light to it with a candle.

Then, just to be on the safe side, he flung the blazing remains out of the window, where it disappeared under the heavy end of a passing steamroller.

Dickens stared down at the results of his efforts in horrified disbelief. He had only meant to stun the intruder. But surely, he reasoned, there wasn't a court in the land that would condemn the over-exuberance of his actions. With a great sigh of relief, he sank into his favourite armchair. The chair shifted beneath his weight, and a voice murmured in his ear:

'Mornington Crescent!'

Dickens leapt to his feet and spun round. The armchair rose, tossing aside its loose covers to reveal…

Dickens grabbed wildly for the clenched teeth. 'Dodgson!' he hissed through them, paling audibly.

'The same,' replied his visitor, removing the anti-macassar from his head with an airy gesture. 'And may I point out that, not only have you lost the game, but believe me, after what I have just witnessed in this room, you are finished, sir. Done for, sir! And that's a fact, sir.'

With a ghastly moan, Dickens clutched his temples and fell to the floor, stone cold mad.

As for Dodgson, full of pride and a sense of his own unchallenged eminence, he returned to his rooms at Oxford and wrote 'The Hunting of the Snark', the dullest comic poem in the English tongue. And that was the end of him. So, in a way, nobody won.

§ § § §

GREAT PLAYERS OF THE GAME
ADMIRAL LORD NELSON [1758–1805]

IT IS well known that Admiral Lord Nelson and his best friend Lady Emma Hamilton kept up a postal game of Mornington Crescent during his long campaigns at sea. Each move could take several months to pass from one player to the next, so in a real sense it was a precursor of the game we know and play today. What is less well known is that Nelson's devotion to the Game had not gone unnoticed by the French, who attempted to exploit this perceived weakness at the Battle of Trafalgar.

When Nelson's flagship made signal before the engagement: 'England expects that every Englishman this day should do his duty', the French flagship responded immediately with the taunting signal: 'Rayners Lane'. Nelson immediately ordered his Flag Lieutenant, Jacob Bunting, to make signal: 'Waterloo'. The French, aggravated by Nelson's bold and insulting riposte, shot him. As the great hero lay expiring on the poop, he breathed a stunningly cunning counter-tack carronade shift – 'Kensal Rise'. 'What did he say?' demanded the ship's surgeon, S. Maturin, of Captain Hardy, in whose arms the Admiral was cradled. 'I believe he said, "Kiss me, Hardy,"' replied the Captain, moistening his lips. And so a legend was born as another legend died.

LETTERS TO THE CHAIRMAN: 2

Dear Humph,

<u>Mornington Crescent</u>

The use of the 'Original Modern' rules in last Saturday's broadcast produced a game which, in my humble opinion, was up to 'International' standard. Please stick to these rules in future, it will be so useful to the amateur game.

If Tim Brooke-Taylor consulted page 28 of the current *Twonk's Almanac*, he would see that the 'Modern' rules date from 1925 whereas the 'Original Modern' appeared on 4th April 1922. This should stop his continual carping.

Yours truly,

Roy Hamsay

Harrow-Weald, Middx.

● *Sadly, you miss the point entirely. The edition of Twonk's you cite contains a misprint on page 28 in the section devoted to the Morden rules. Incidentally, on the subject of misprints, Brooke-Taylor has obtained some tablets from his doctor, and the trouble has settled down quite satisfactorily.*

Humph

Dear Mr Lyttelton,

Without mentioning any names, the constant whinging and carping by Tim Brooke-Taylor the WHOLE time Mornington Crescent is being played is beginning to get me down. In the forties, during the blackout, down in the underground, up to 4,000 a night played and there was NEVER any argument. This was because we ALWAYS stuck rigidly to the rules laid down by the Marquis of Turbery *(sic)*. Oh please, PLEASE, before I die, could I hear the game played once more to the Turbery (*sic*) rules, to remind me of happier times gone by when life was civilised and genteel in the war?

Yours sincerely,
Mrs Pat Penegar
New Milton, Hants

Dear Mrs Penegar
You are not alone in yearning for the old values which the Marquess of Turberry came to represent to admirers of the game. However, one has only to look to the history of 'Mornington Crescent' in this country to discover a catalogue of fights, brawls and drunken, loutish behaviour that attended some of the higher-profile games. Christopher Marlowe himself, it has now been suggested, was murdered after attempting a dubious triangulation from Holborn to Finchley Central (as it is now called). How history repeats itself.

Jon Naismith, Producer, *I'm Sorry I Haven't A Clue*

Dear Mr Naismith,
I am afraid I cannot agree at all about your reference to Christopher Marlowe. If it is called Finchley Central now, surely it was called the same thing then.

Yours sincerely, Pat Penegar (Mrs)
P.S. Why can't Humphrey Lyttelton write his own letters – lazy git.

● *Naismith doesn't know what he's talking about. Incidentally, are you by any chance related to Gustav Penegar, of Penegar's Principles of Congruence? I had the pleasure of knowing him slightly. Now he was a lazy git. Humph.*

MORNINGTON CRESCENT
SYMBOL, SECRECY AND CODE

THE TURKS

It would seem to have been from the Turks that we ultimately inherited the basis of the Modern Game. The Sultan Othman, original architect of the Ottoman Empire, famously enjoyed playing the game while taking sherbet, and the habit soon spread. History relates that Seljuk Sultan Alaudin was so fond of Mornington Crescent that he formerly adopted the crescent symbol as a badge for the Ottoman Empire. Even today it can still be seen adorning the Turkish flag.

THE KNIGHTS TEMPLAR

After delivering Jerusalem from the infidel, a small band of crusaders united to form a secret society, intent on the spread of their three abiding passions: religious fervour, martial prowess and Mornington Crescent. Undoubtedly they developed the last of these obsessions from captured Turks who they had to torture, often brutally, in order to learn the rules. From thence, this primitive form of Mornington Crescent (or 'Deeb Dhab' as translated phonetically from the original Turkish) was imported to France, together with the accompanying sherbet. Like their Turkish tutors, The Knights Templar took a solemn vow never to betray the process behind their sacred game. All that now remains of their secret legacy are a few standard progressions (All Saints – Angel – Hatton Cross), a handy triangulation (Temple – St

Paul's – St Pancras – Temple again), and the novels of Leslie Charteris, whose coded adventures of Simon 'Templar' will have provided some consolation at least for any remaining crusader knights.

THE FREEMASONS

Mornington Crescent has been a prominent feature of many of the world's most secret societies. In the early Middle Ages, the itinerant stonemasons who laid the cornerstones of London's original street plan were superb tacticians of the Ancient Standard game. Unlike the majority of the British population, whose bonded serfdom meant they seldom strayed more than a few miles from their homes, the stonemasons were the first real journeymen. Their architect's training and natural facility with angles, combined with an uncanny geographical sense, gave them an almost superhuman advantage over less well-travelled

Masonic Lodge meeting in full Mornington Crescent regalia.

players of the game. As these medieval masons inevitably developed their own secret society, so began their quest for an effective system of codes. Increasingly, the distinctive funny handshake was mistakenly interpreted as a schoolyard prank (even among fellow members), and wearers of the extraordinary masonic apron dress were frequently being confused with

The National Paving Stone Archive at Mornington Crescent.

Morris dancers. It took the London mason and cartographer Herbert Harold Ordinance to develop a series of 'move sequences' that would hold a secret meaning for experienced players. For example: 'Bayswater – Redbridge – Ickenham – Brixton – Edmonton' could immediately be interpreted as an incentive to assist a fellow freemason, while 'Tottenham – Old Street – Shoreditch – Edgware – Rotherhithe' was a useful term of abuse.

THE WAR

Come the dawn of the 20th century and the outbreak of war in Europe, the need for an effective code system had become increasingly imperative. Perhaps due to the number of masons in high office at the time, the preferred system was created from the five quarterly move cycles involved in the alternative British Standard version of Mornington Crescent. Depending on whether the game was elliptical or progressional, lateral or inverted, the multiples of play were so vast that a single code could be translated into at least seven languages. Naturally the Germans were dumbfounded, and not a single message was ever decoded during the length of World War II. Indeed, so secure was the code that it is highly doubtful whether our own codebreakers would have been able to understand it either.

German Paratroopers.

MORNINGTON CRESCENT
A HISTORY OF THE GAME

PART 5 **THE LEGACY OF EMPIRE**

One of the greatest curiosities for the travelling man is to observe quite how far the game of Mornington Crescent has travelled. From the tea-growing heights of Darjeeling to the sugar plantations of the Caribbean, Mornington Crescent has been translated into 72 languages, sixteen romantic novels, seven stage plays, three art-house films and a Brazilian street carnival.

In the Marshall Islands of the South Pacific it has been worshipped for several centuries, and up until the 1940s, visitors to the beautiful Bikini Atoll could see for themselves the sacred shrine to the underground station erected by natives. In 1954 however, the United States detonated a 15-megaton H-bomb there, and the shrine, together with three

The beach bar at Bikini Atoll.

neighbouring islands, was sadly vaporised, its radioactive remains deposited over a radius of 50,000 square miles.

It is perhaps unsurprising that Mornington Crescent has been seen by many British colonies as a cruel instrument of Empire. The history of the West Indies relates how the terrified indigenous population looked on helplessly as the invading British torched all the icons, symbols, dice, sawdust and spanking-paddles associated with their native game 'Stump', forcing the bewildered islanders to substitute them for the unfamiliar London street names of the Straight Standard Game. Most did eventually take to the new pastime, but the conversion was not absolute. Tourists still report sightings of remote hill tribes playing an unusual variation. Thomas Cook was witness to one such game. He wrote: 'The game these men are playing would not be recognised at home. As far as I can distinguish, Arnos Grove is wild, Junkin's Progression is completely ignored, Euston Road is deemed a Vertical Approach(!), and any player unlucky enough to find himself blocked after an elliptical progression is doused in honey, rolled in sawdust and beaten about the thighs and buttocks with little wooden butter pats.'

Mahatma Gandhi's famous Two Hundred Mile March of 1930 to expose the injustice of British Home Rule in India, in a brilliantly ironic touch, followed a route to mimic Lord Grosvenor's even then outdated Principles of Triangulation.

There are tribes in Papua New Guinea which only play Mornington Crescent after consuming the roots of the kava-kava plant, famed for its narcotic

A native aborigine proudly displays the twin crescent shapes on his buttocks to denote that he has recently sat on a freshly painted park bench.

properties. Players apparently chew the kava-kava root until a state of paranoid psychosis is achieved, before attempting Thornton's Standard Deviation *without* tagging.

On many of the smaller Fijian Islands, natives have played Mornington Crescent to elect their local government representatives. Play is to the best of fifteen games, the outright winners being duly elected. Many consider this process considerably more reliable than a conventional democratic election, which may go some way to explaining the instability of the national government in recent years.

In Albania, after independence from Turkey was achieved in 1927 and a republic proclaimed, the people were given a free vote to nominate their king. After several re-counts, a tie was announced between C. B. Fry, the distinguished cricketer, and Arthur Allbright, the Mornington Crescent grand master and first exponent of Allbright's now famous Opening. A cricketing tour of Ceylon was to rule Fry out, so it was Allbright who eventually acceded to the Albanian throne. To international surprise, he led the Albanian people with considerable success for quite a few weeks, until ill-advisedly issuing a public proclamation that Tooting Bec was inadmissible after the Central Line had been Quartered. In the ensuing coup, he was hurriedly put to death and King Zog was crowned in his stead.

And in remote Pitcairn Island, recent archaeological explorations have unearthed husks of several half-eaten breadfruit, upon which appear to have been carved lengthy scorecards for a game of Mornington Crescent which seems to have lasted for several months. They tell us that the Tahitian women effectively sealed the fate of the mutineers after cleverly sacrificing Beak Street at a crucial intersection, thereby closing down their opponents' vertical and horizontal approaches. Sweet revenge I should imagine.

Supporters of the Touring Team eagerly await news of the West Indian score.

DID ALIEN COMMUTERS ONCE TRAVEL AMONG US?
EXTRACTS FROM THE BOOK MORNINGTON CRESCENT OF THE GODS

[Heineken Paperbooks £11.99]
By Herbert van Luniken

Yes, it's true! Alien Visitors from Other Worlds have really and truly visited Our Planet in the Dim and Distant Passed! Against All the Odds, I have compelling proof of this Astounding Fact. Many of my so-called 'critics' (most of them distinguished and highly-qualified scientists) have pooh-poohed on my theories, but that is just where they are wrong. My evidence is incontroversial, and when they kick up a stink they only shoot themselves in his own feet! Mornington Crescent is without doubt not of earthly origin. You want proof? There is proof a-plenty, and lots of it too. Look no further than Stone Henge!

Stonehenge

Here we are at Stone Henge, a mysterious 'henge' or 'tourist attraction' – a strange and eary group of stones that sits breeding astride Salisbury Plains. What a gloomy place! But why oh why oh why did our four bears struggle to arouse this erection those forty countless centuries ago? My observations conclusively prove that the layout is uncannily similar like Piccadilly Circus Tube Station, with the arches matching precisely the number of arched entrances of the modern structure. Be kind to remember too that

Groundforce visits Stonehenge.

Stone Henge was originally buried deep under the grounds, as if this were not proof enough for the septic!

The Pyramids

Look at the Pyramids! OK you have to go to Egypt to do this, but it is, well, worth the effort. What do they remind you of, apart from other pyramids? Yes, me too! They are laid out in the self-same pattern like the stations from Gloucester Road to Green Park in the 'Green Park Triangle', which you will not forget is bounded by Earls Court, Westminster, and Bond Street. Moreover, the Pyramids are made of triangles – and how do you progress from Gloucester Road to Green Park when Stought's Proscription is in force? Why, by triangulation of course! And what do all these mentions of triangles tot up to? We have all heard the rumours that Stought was secretly an Egyptian, but was he also an Alien? Perhaps he was. I call it eary!

The Bible Code

Take the Bible down from your shelf and open it at the Book of Genesis, which comes at the front. I will now reveal to you the mysterious code which I discovered locked within this centuries-old text, which goes a long way to proving my thesis. On a piece of scrap paper [you will find plenty enclosed in this book] print the name 'MORNINGTON CRESCENT' and assign a number to each letter according to its place in the alphabet: M-13, O-15, R-18, N-14, I-9, and so fourth. Now for the exciting bit! Count to the 13th letter of the Good Book [the Bible, that is, not this one, although this is also a good book but in a different way!] and note it down – you'll find it's the final 'N' in 'beginning'. Then count 15 letters on from this one [H] then 18 letters on from that one [N] then 14 letters on from that one [I] and so on until the eary cryptic message is revealed. You will be as astounded as everyone else to discover that the hidden message is as thus: 'NHIAN U AF OFE SEEW GEN'*

Proof, if any more were needed, that Alien Visitors had once visited our most ancient transport system, leaving behind a note to future generations, and what's more – they spoke Welsh!

*'*Please mind the gap.*'

Easter Island

Like eary giants the gigantic stone heads rise upwards from the grounds on Easter Island. It sends a shiver through our marrows. Were they put there by Alien hands as a message to us, or as an aid to navigation, or as garden ornaments, or are they a hint to the rules of the Universal Game? We may never know the answer for sure, but careful measurements and calculations have thrown up a grand surprise. Each and every one of those gigantic giant heads stares in silent vigil in the precise direction of Finsbury Park.

The Nazca Lines

What is the secret of the enormous map of the Northern Line etched into the deserted wastes of the Nazca Desert in Peru? It can only be seen from Outer Space, or from a low-flying helicopter. The early Native Mayans had no helicopters, so you are permitted to draw your own conclusions. Nearby there is a cluster of tombstones next to a ruined Chapel of Rest and a Crematorium, which may be an ancient burial site. Carved into a stone is the figure of a 'priest', but by screwing up your eyes you can imagine it to be the form of an eary commuter holding onto an overhead strap trying to read the newspaper. Need I go on?

GREAT PLAYERS OF THE GAME
AIR VICE-MARSHALL DOUGLAS 'DUMPER' WALLACE [1859–1962]

DOUGLAS 'Dumper' Wallace was a welcome fixture around many of the bridge tables and nightclub dance floors during and immediately after the war. His recklessness in play was matched only by his exuberant deployment of the aggressive 'all-or-nothing' tactics, which often cowed his opponents, and even many of his team-mates, into submission. With a wild cry of 'Tally-hoo!' he would launch some madcap frontal assault on Upminster Bridge or Snaresbrook, forcing a perilous Hooking Volley within the Diagonal with inevitable results.

'Dumper's many fans found it hard to believe that he came to the Game so late in life, but the socialite war hero was a latecomer in almost everything he turned his hand to. At the age of 81 he was the oldest pilot to fly Spitfires during World War II, and despite failing eyesight he played an important part in the Battle of Brixton. He was in his eighties at the time, and his hearing was not what it was – this perhaps accounts for the fact that he carried out the order to bomb the armament factories in Dresden by single-handedly destroying an ornament factory in Harlesden. Miraculously surviving a fatal prang after mistaking a tall broadcasting aerial for the Battleship Graf Spee, his exploits were recorded in the motion picture *Ice Cold in Alexandra Palace*, which earned him a new generation of admirers.

After serving briefly on Churchill's war staff, where he is credited with coining the phrase 'D-Day', thanks to his slight but unmistakable stutter, 'Dumper' went on to lead Bomber Command on their first and unsuccessful 'bouncing bomb' mission to destroy the East and West Hams. His glorious flying career came to a premature end when it came to light that a clerical error had led to his accidental promotion to Air Vice-Marshall, and his actual rank was bosun's mate in the Merchant Navy. Nevertheless he was allowed to retain 'Air Vice-Marshall' as a courtesy title, by special dispensation, and put in charge of in-flight catering for Fighter Command.

He is fondly remembered by his many friends, who treasure the endless fund of reminiscences with which he would regale them in his later years. 'I had a good war,' he would often remark, usually five or six times a minute.

'Keep up at the back'. Dumper third from left.

MORNINGTON CRESCENT
A GLOSSARY OF TERMS

Albright's Opening – Totteridge & Whetstone.

Aldgate – gate in a west-facing wall, from the Old Norse 'ald' [west] 'gyatt' [door].

Aldgate East – an east-facing Ald-gyatt.

Alexandra Palace – first female BBC announcer to introduce an edition of 'Hats off to Mornington Crescent!' – 1947.

All Saints – popular music combo whose members once worked as Tube Hostesses on the Northern Line.

Alperton – small sour eating apple, now banned under EC directive 4756AL/P.

Amersham – type of rough woven cloth used for sailors' handkerchiefs.

Angel – Theatrical backer [vulg. slang].

Armitage Shanks Charity Bowl, The – presented to the winner of UK Domestic League grand final.

Arnos Grove – first BBC announcer to host 'Hats off to Mornington Crescent!', Home Service, 1936.

Barbican – Tube of Foster's.

Barking – original site of Bedlam.

Barkingside – the dogs' home next to Bedlam.

Beckton Park – second BBC announcer to host 'Hats off to Mornington Crescent!', 1937.

Blackfriars – a mendicant order of monks who walked the Pilgrim's Loop from Beacontree to Morden.

Bounds Green – an unlocking move which renders all Bounding Advances open.

Brighton Handicap, The – in which the lateral shift can be employed to box opponents out of the game. However, once Tooting Bec has been declared, the move is disallowed unless two or more players are in nip. George IV popularised the

Brighton Handicap, which he is said to have picked up while visiting the town on his holidays.

Canary Wharf – a respiratory disease of cage birds.

Chancery Lane – third BBC radio announcer to host 'Hats off to Mornington Crescent!', 1939.

Clapham Common – a butterfly.

Cockfosters – agricultural workers who replace cockerels.

Colindale – the Sell-Winton Academy of Music.

Dagenham Heathway – fourth BBC radio announcer to host 'Hats off to Mornington Crescent!', 1940.

Dalston Kingsland – fifth and last BBC radio announcer to host 'Hats off to Mornington Crescent!', 1941.

Epping – small rodent living in underground burrows.

Fairlop – small single-masted brigantine, first used around Fairlop Docks.

Finchley Road & Frognal – firm of solicitors.

Freud, Sigmund – (1856–1939) is known to have used Mornington Crescent as an alternative to word association.

Gipsy Hill – travelling soccer pundit.

Gray's Anatomy – biological textbook by Henry Gray (1827–1861), used by medical students for extreme variant set within the human body. Play terminates at the pancreas (or St Pancreas) without traversing the major arteries. Apparently provided Dr Graeme Garden with his first real experience of the game.

Harrow & Wealdstone – agricultural implements *c.* eighteenth century, used for skeaping rushes between 5 and 6 pm ['the rush hour'].

Heathrow Terminals 1, 2, 3, 4 – children's counting rhyme.

Hornchurch – Chapel of the Blessed St Humphrey, in Tilbury Docks.

Hugo's Parabola – the perfect curved move. Still not mathematically proven.

Hugo's 2nd Stratagem – moves across consecutive rows are prohibited.

Johnson, Dr – (1709–1784) renowned amateur player of the game, who is supposed to have declared: 'When a man is tired of Mornington Crescent, he'll change at Euston and get off at Camden Town.'

Knaresborough Rules – a variation brought to Yorkshire by Lord Knaresborough. When a player has been blocked he is in 'Nidd', which involves the forfeit of three moves. Great fun!

Lifts & Escalators – a bastardised variation in which play begins at Fairlop. In the unlikely situation that players land on a station with operational lift service, they must immediately return to Fairlop. If they land on an escalator however, they are quickly catapulted to Chalk Farm Road.

Luton – Japanese couch which converts into another couch.

Marble Arch – painful condition of the feet, caused by overuse of escalators.

Martello Convention, The – (1807) formerly authorised use of the Broadside Turn (whereby a player can repeat his opponent's declaration and thereby reverse the order of player). The convention was welcomed, especially by sailors, who responded positively to the legitimisation of sudden diagonal play to starboard ('tacking') and the fact that when a player is blocked they are in 'poop' and should miss a turn.

Marylebone – 'Honeymoon priapism' [vulg. slang].

Morningside Crescent – refined Scottish version. Shunting and straddling are considered unacceptable.

Mornington Crescent – a game.

Mornington Crescent Phone-ins – from the invention of the telephone, unscrupulous racketeers have taken advantage of public gullibility. Lonely players have made calls to the many 0898 chatlines promising late-night games, only to find the charges extortionate and the standard of play extremely variable.

Mornington Croissant – a French variation, based on the famous Metro system in Newcastle. Usually played over breakfast.

Mornington Royal Crescent (Bath) – a clever eighteenth-century variation that is seldom played nowadays due to the emphasis on cyclical play, which means games can drag on interminably. Trumps are conventional.

Morton's Convention – horizontal play is only permissible when a pursuant has been huffed. Mainline stations are of course wild.

Morton's Second Parallel – if two parallel moves follow consecutively, the order of play is automatically reversed.

Mudchute – [vulg. slang].

Nash Convention, The – see Regency Rules.

Northern League version – popularised by the monks of Kirkstall Abbey. Cloistering is only allowed after Kensal Rise has been played. A slow move runs the risk of a penalty for the guilty player: he must remain silent for two moves. Some monasteries permitted him to write his moves during this penalty period and submit them to a referee.

Ockendon – treble 19 at darts.

Ongar – dish of eels stewed in gruel, popular among ticket inspectors.

Osterley – dull, peevish, ill-tempered.

Parsons Green – ointment for warts.

Pimlico – a clown operating on public transport.

Pinner – Carriage-cleaner's snack.

Plaistow – a soft form of bakelite.

Poplar – man-made fibre. Poplarisation – making shirts from wood.

Quex Road – a controversial Supine Congress from Hatch End.

Radlett – dish of cheese and root vegetables.

Rainham – edible transparent plastic hat-cover.

Regency Rules – see the Nash Convention.

Reverse Mornington Crescent – a highly exacting variation in which the first player actually starts at Mornington Crescent, after which each subsequent player has to deduce what the previous move would have been to have arrived in that position, and so on until the first move is identified by the winner. (For practice purposes, a perfect template is probably the 1974 Eastern Bloc semi-final in Gdansk between Zloti and Kipf, played to Standard Regulations, which Kipf won with a call of Kings Cross after two hours and 36 minutes.)

Rickmansworth – a jobbing actor.

Royal & Ancient Rules (Scotland) – anyone forced out of bounds is required to take the nearest playable station, usually Charing Cross. Water hazards are likely to incur a dropped turn so look out when passing water. Players can still 'stymie' an opponent by blocking his passage.

Seven Sisters – group of massive limestone rocks at the southernmost tip of Uxbridge platform.

Shoeburyness – a state of discomfort, accompanied by a desire for the floor to open and swallow one up.

Soho Square – removed by the Victorians. Still disallowed in the censored version of the game.

Speed Mornington Crescent – chiefly the preserve of the showman, due both to the strict time limit imposed between moves, as well as the suspension of all blindside boundaries. As you can imagine, in the hands of experienced players, it can be breathtaking to watch. The World Speed Mornington Crescent record stands at 17.2 seconds* and was achieved by two Finns – Jorgen Matte and Jan Neilsen – in 1982. They also recorded a time of 18.1 seconds at altitude. The UK record is currently 1 minute 2.45 seconds, which gives us a ranking of 17 – not very impressive considering our natural advantage. Calls still continue for the game to be taught more in schools. *Based on a six-move permutation.*

St John's Wood – a holy relic; a part of the genuine Charing Cross.

Stamford Brook – first BBC radio announcer to introduce 'Mornington Crescent – Hoorah!', 1945.

Standard Deviation, The – perhaps the purest form of the game. The nib holder may play advantage after a looped move, which means it's probably best to avoid Fairlop altogether.

Stanford-le-Hope – See Winchmore Hill.

Stovold, N. F. – author of *Mornington Crescent: Rules & Origins*, considered by many to be the most comprehensive text ever written about the game. Sadly out of print.

Tagging – a player follows the preceding move with a straight sequential in an attempt to trap the opposition in a repeating loop.

Theydon Bois – melodramatic actor, most famous for his role as 'Ickenham' in *Terror at Mornington Crescent*, 1954.

Totteridge & Whetstone – legendary music-hall double act, remembered vaguely for their comical song: 'I lost my potater on the down escalator!'

Tudor Court Rules (sixteenth century) – a version known to have been played by Henry VIII and possibly Shakespeare. Basically identical to the modern game, but with a considerably smaller playing area. Stovold records this rather eccentric by-law from the time: 'At the passing of the cod piece, 'tis the holder who may nominate, except when out of croup.'

Turberry, Marquess of – Hugo Granville Kolpoise Smith, 87th Marquess of Turberry (1837–1899). Formulated the Turberry Rules (referred to now as Original Modern Rules). An all-round boardgame player, Turberry's particular enthusiasm was 'Mornington Crescent'. Alarmed by the increasing number of duelling fatalities (the result of many arguments over what were then highly uncertain rules), Turberry determined to set out a basic code of 'principles of play', many of which still survive to this day. Turberry's name was to become synonymous with good sportsmanship, and though by no means a great player of the game, huge crowds would come to admire the grace and dignity he displayed in defeat. The greatest test on Turberry's reserves of dignity was to come after he mistakenly accused the dramatist and critic George Bernard Shaw of homosexuality. The charge was to rebound on him when at the subsequent court hearing the judge concluded that it was in fact Turberry himself who was the homosexual. Fleeing to Tangiers, Turberry lived out the last few years of his life, quietly developing his basic set of ground rules for gay relationships. Even to this day, you can ask for a 'Turberry' at any lay-by, heath, common, or gay cruising area. You'll be greatly rewarded for the trouble.

Twonk, Tobias – (1599–1648) Amateur astronomer and calligrapher who in 1621 produced the very first Mornington Crescent Almanac. Covering every league game in the country and most international tournaments, early editions were simply too heavy for a single man to carry and copies were transported via an elaborate system of rollers. Though slow at first, sales really took off in 1640 when the double-column print format was developed and the book's marble binding was replaced with leather. Constant study of the night sky was to have a debilitating effect on Twonk's eyesight, an explanation perhaps for the considerable number of misprints for which the book has become norotious.

Old Twonk's Almanac is now in its 302nd edition.

Upminster – a card game, involving two full packs of cards and a spanner.

Upminster Bridge – a refined version of Upminster, involving two spanners and a bowl.

Upney – a Cockney from Highgate.

Varsity Rules – still played by Oxbridge undergraduates. 'Colleging' and 'bumping' are permissible, but only on the diagonal.

Vauxhall – [vulg. slang].

Virtual Reality Mornington Crescent – a Taiwanese gimmick of the late eighties. The cumbersome helmets and disappointing graphics made it a non-starter, except in Belgium.

Wapping – a disease of sheep.

Waterloo – Thomas Crapper's prototype closet.

Watling Street Variation, The – players can only take the direct route between any two given points, so looped moves are disallowed and the Circle Line is out of bounds. Players may huff as much as they like.

Wimbledon – a parasitic fly.

Winchmore Hill – only Director General of the BBC to have taken part in a public round of Mornington Crescent. [Beaten by Stanford le-Hope, 1961.]

Windsor Rules – as you'd expect from the name, this variant has links to organised crime in the East End of London. Only the senior player in a straight line may inherit possession, unless of course the Hapsburg Connection has been invoked, in which case Grimaldi's Protocol takes precedence.

SELECT BIBLIOGRAPHY

PRINTED SOURCES

Dimbleby, Richard, *Nightmares On The Job* (Heinemann Press, 1953)

Gyles, B. R. and Ret, H., *Cribbage Explained* (Ladybird, 1971)

Knaresborough, Lord, *Peepholes & Paramours – The Confessional Diaries* (London, 1799 – banned)

Lawrence, T. E., *The Seven Pillows Of Willesden* (Abu Dhabi, 1937)

Lee Potter, Linda, *The Really Useful Reference Book on Mornington Crescent* (Daily Mail Publications, 1988)

Orwell, George, *Down And Out In London And Three Moves* (Penguin, 1957)

Rushdie, Sally-Anne, *Rebecca Of Surrey Quays Farm* (Oxford, 1981)

Sell, Colin, *The World's Worst Music Hall Songs* (Vanity Press, 1992)

Smith, Delia, *Cooking For Commuters* (BBC, 1975)

Smith, Delia, *The London Cook's A–Z* (BBC, 1976)

Stovold, N. F., *Mornington Crescent: Rules & Origins* (London, 1757)

Turberry, Marquess of, *The Art of Losing* (London, 1879)

Twonk, Tobias, *The Almanac, Volumes I–XXV* (London, 1637)

Vorderman, Carol, *Mornington Crescent From M to C* (Cambridge, 1992)

MAGAZINES

Gentleman's Quarterly, Sept. 1892, vol. 27

Good Housekeeping, Feb. 1987

GQ, March 1997

Railwayman's Gazette, Vols XII–XX

Which Witch, No. VII (1575)

SONGS

Bowie, David, 'Station To Station', 1976

McTell, Ralph, 'The Streets of London', 1974

Stevens, Cat, 'Mornington Crescent (Like The First Morning)', 1972

INDEX